Praise for
When Parenting Isn't Perfect

Jim Daly has done a great job in reminding parents that perfection is not only unattainable but harmful in the journey of parenting. God's grace is available in abundance for good reason: we all need it. Perfectionism is slow suicide!

DR. KEVIN LEMAN, *New York Times* bestselling
author of *Have a New Kid by Friday*

This book is long overdue. Many moms and dads today are beating themselves up because they are not perfect. This book shows parenting for what it is—imperfect. It highlights the beauty of imperfection and lets parents off the hook, so that they can focus on the tangible truths and realities of parenting. A must-read for every parent. My friend Jim Daly has not only nailed this topic; I've seen him live it out with his own children.

MITCH TEMPLE, licensed marriage and
family therapist, author, and executive director
of The Fatherhood Commission

As the president of Focus on the Family, Jim Daly lives and breathes parenting, and he truly understands the challenges parents face today. In *When Parenting Isn't Perfect*, Jim has written a book that all parents, regardless of their season of life, are and will be high-fiving about, since they all know it's true: perfect parenting is just not possible.

BRAD LOMENICK, former president of Catalyst
and author of *H3 Leadership* and *The Catalyst Leader*

As a parent, I know it's easy to feel alone in your worries, shortcomings, and failures, assuming that everyone else has it all together. In this incredibly timely book, Jim Daly offers a much-needed shot of grace to stressed-out parents everywhere and reminds all of us that *messy* is often perfectly okay, and even beautiful, in God's eyes. *When Parenting Isn't Perfect* is an absolute must-read for families everywhere.

REV. SAMUEL RODRIGUEZ, president of the National
Hispanic Christian Leadership Conference (NHCLC)

WHEN
PARENTING
ISN'T
PERFECT

Also by Jim Daly

Marriage Done Right: One Man, One Woman

The Good Dad: Becoming the Father You Were Meant to Be

ReFocus: Living a Life That Reflects God's Heart

Stronger: Trading Brokenness for Unbreakable Strength

Finding Home: An Imperfect Path to Faith and Family

WHEN
PARENTING
ISN'T
PERFECT

JIM DALY

WITH PAUL ASAY

ZONDERVAN®

ZONDERVAN

*To parents everywhere
who love their children
and want their hearts rooted in Christ*

CONTENTS

FOREWORD

I first met Jim Daly quite soon after he had become president of Focus on the Family. I had flown in to do a series of radio broadcasts at the ministry headquarters, and Jim asked to meet before the recordings began. Since I didn't know much about him, I was curious about him. I was aware he had a lot of pressure on him to perform at high levels in his new role.

Within a few minutes, I remember thinking, *I could hang out with this guy*. He was real and vulnerable. Authentic. There was zero attitude. In fact, he was telling stories on himself where he came out looking like a fool, and he'd laugh his head off. I was quickly drawn to Jim's "realness."

That meeting fostered a friendship that has lasted for many years and through many radio broadcasts. In fact, Jim is now a Fellow of the Townsend Institute, and a very popular one.

In addition to the friendship, however, I deeply respect Jim's thoughts, writings, and speaking. I have shared keynote speaking stages with him and have greatly benefited from his books. Jim researches his topics thoroughly and biblically, and he writes from his own experience. And Jim's writing is who he is—authentic and "himself." You can trust what he writes because he doesn't mind showing the reader how he has grown and changed. Most of us have a difficult time reading authors who always appear to have it all together.

Because of who Jim is, I can't think of anyone more suited to write a parenting book about dealing with our imperfections in that role. Jim's authenticity and vulnerability come through as he describes learning from his own mistakes as a parent. As readers, we immediately come out of the "shame attack" that all of us parents feel, in areas where we have made so many mistakes with our kids. Jim normalizes imperfection, shows us how to deal with it, and moves on to offer solutions for parenting problems. The chapter titled "Not Good Enough" alone is worth the price of the book.

What an important book for any parent to read today! We are always assessing ourselves to see if we parent well:

- Am I spending enough time with my children?
- Am I listening and encouraging well?
- Am I not strict enough, or am I too strict?
- Is there a guarantee that I won't royally damage my kids?

Our culture and the media don't provide a lot of answers. But Jim offers many healthy ways to support our children's growth "in the nurture and admonition of the Lord" (Ephesians 6:4 KJV) and from a position of *grace and acceptance* for the parent.

What a relief to read a balanced book with valuable ideas that helps the reader be the kind of grace-filled parent Jim writes about— the kind of parent who courageously embraces the great adventure of parenting. Thanks, Jim, for a brilliant contribution.

JOHN TOWNSEND,
New York Times bestselling author of *Boundaries*,
psychologist, and founder of the Townsend
Institute for Leadership and Counseling

PROLOGUE

I learned about family between commercials.

My mother was hardly ever around when I got home from school. As a single mom keeping five kids fed and clothed, she worked a lot—often from ten in the morning to eleven at night. My dad wasn't around. And my brothers and sisters, all older than me, were off doing other stuff. I was a latchkey kid before anyone had a name for it.

Most days, then, I came home to an empty house. Just me and the TV.

And so television became my childhood companion. After returning home from school, I'd close the door, pull a Cactus Cooler out of the fridge, flip on the television, and plop down on the floor—tummy on the carpet, feet banging against the couch, my hand within easy reach of the dial. And for an hour or two, I'd join another, better family. A family where parents hugged and advised and gently scolded their kids, where even the biggest problems could get solved before bedtime.

Great, loving families filled the television screen back when I grew up in the 1960s and '70s. Bill Davis and his butler, Giles French, raised his orphaned nieces and nephew in CBS's *Family Affair*. Widower Steven Douglas gently taught his trio of boys in *My Three Sons*. In *The Brady Bunch* (an avant-garde creation, since it depicted a blended family), architect and widower Mike Brady marries widow Carol Ann

Martin, combining their collective brood of three daughters and three sons into one of television's most beloved families.

These were the most "normal" families I knew—nearly the only constants I had for much of my childhood. (Yes, I joined Marcia Brady's fan club.) These shows gave me a healthier perspective of what families *should* look like. I found elements in them I could relate to and take comfort from. We became a blended family for a while, just like *The Brady Bunch*. Then when I lost my mom, I took solace in the fact that the boys in *My Three Sons* had no mother either.

These families resembled mine, but seemed better. More reassuring. Mike and Carol Brady always had the right answers. Steven Douglas never got drunk. Bill Davis cared for his nieces and nephews as if they were his very own children. Amazing. On television, it seemed like the families on the small screen always did things well. They did things the *right* way.

And sometimes, I wondered why my own family didn't.

Today, I wonder how many other families back then might've looked at those perfect TV moms and dads and thought the same thing. How many moms listened to their screaming kids and asked themselves, "Where did I go wrong?" How many dads left for work feeling guilty, and yet with a sense of relief? How many kids wished their parents would solve the family's problems with a knowing smile and a laugh track instead of through yelling and spanking and maybe worse?

The Brady clan vanished from television a long time ago, of course. No father on TV knows best anymore. But we still chase that telegenic ideal. We know what a perfect family looks like. We know what ours looks like. And we wonder why we see such a difference between the two.

Do you know the easy answer to this question of *why*? It's *because*. Because we're different. We're flawed. We're human. No one scripts our family lives for us. No director yells "cut!" if we say the wrong thing. To ask why your family is no better than it is—why my family isn't better—is maybe the entirely wrong question to ask.

So instead of asking why, let's ask *how*. How can our families be better? How can we fix our broken relationships and make them whole again? How can we overcome our inevitable mistakes and create healthy, safe environments for our kids—and for us parents too?

I haven't written a book about finding perfection. I've written one about finding the beauty in imperfection—and how that beauty reflects God's own relationship with us. I write about avoiding dysfunction while embracing the occasional family mess.

This book won't turn your family into the Brady Bunch! But it will help you deal with truth and reality. If you're already doing family well, this book will help you embrace your blessings and build empathy for those families who struggle with love, grace, and truth.

PART ONE

✦

How Good Is Good Enough?

Chapter One

NOT GOOD ENOUGH

✦

How easily we all slip into the trap of thinking that we're working toward perfection. We put so much pressure on ourselves and our families, even though that very pressure conflicts with what Jesus talked about during his days on earth. We equate living a good Christian life with living a sinless life. We try so hard to be righteous on our own when Jesus has already told us, *You're not going to make it. That's why I died for you.*

Yes, Jesus died for us, but we all still keep score. We're living like good Pharisees. It's as though we've forgotten to read our Bibles. Or if we are reading them, we're not paying close enough attention to apply its teachings to our lives. How many verses talk about our weaknesses and God's strength? How many insist we can't be perfect in this life? How the grace of God is our only hope?

We're weak. We have imperfect families. And yes, by our pharisaical standards, we're not good enough.

And we're right. We're *not* good enough. Not if we measure ourselves by God's holy yardstick. He painted us in His own image; we're the Mona Lisas of His creation, the masterpiece of the universe. But we couldn't leave well enough alone and elected to "improve" the product with fingerpaints. We fall far short of His beautiful design, and we know it; many of our pharisaical tendencies start there. God asks us to return to our original design. God asks us to strive for perfection. And so we try. Oh, how we try.

But instead of trying to be perfect in His eyes, we try to be perfect in our own. We concentrate on our behavior: earning the A's, grabbing the gold stars, saying and doing just the right things to make everyone around us ooh and aah at just how good we are. We forget that God weighs perfection on a much different scale. We think perfection is all about what we *do*; we forget that it's about who we *are*.

As we chase after this solemn, intimidating goal, we forget the grace that runs along with it. In a faith filled with paradox, this may be one of the biggest: God asks us to seek perfection, even though He knows we'll never find it. He loves us, even though we messed up His masterpiece. Sometimes I think we feel even more of His love in the midst of those messes, because that's when we need it the most.

"Be perfect, therefore, as your heavenly Father is perfect," Jesus tells us in Matthew 5:48. Pretty daunting. We give ourselves ulcers trying to be that picture of perfection and to demand that same perfection from the people closest to us.

But why, as we scramble after perfection, do we rarely think of modeling God's perfect grace? His perfect forgiveness? His patient, perfect love?

Because it's far more difficult. We can game a behavioral "A." We can't game character. We have to learn it. Earn it. And sometimes it only comes through suffering.

We're faced with a paradox: While we measure our own perfection through our successes, we develop God's perfection through our misses, mistakes, and even failures.

And sometimes it even develops when those failures pull us away from Him.

Disappointment and Disaster

Casey was nineteen when she got pregnant.

She came from a good Christian home. Books by all the best Christian parenting experts lined her parents' shelves. Mom and Dad monitored the music she listened to, the movies she watched, and the books she read. The whole family ate at the dining room table every night, and she and her mother read the Bible together every morning.

She went off to college—a Christian college—with a sky-high GPA and a strong SAT score. When her parents dropped her off at the dorm, they all cried a little. "You're going to do great things here, honey," her father told her. "Great things." And Casey hoped he spoke the truth. She would do her best to make him proud.

And then she fell in love. Doug, an English major, had the same backstory—good family, high aspirations, solid faith.

They had sex anyway. And all the lessons Casey learned, all the guilt and shame she felt after every tryst, didn't convince her to stop.

She missed her period the spring of her sophomore year. After two weeks, she and Doug walked to a nearby pregnancy center, not telling a soul. The test showed positive.

To Casey, it seemed like the air went cold. She could feel Doug's hand in hers, slick with icy sweat.

"Are you sure?" Doug asked. With a smile meant to be gentle, the clinician handed them some pamphlets—"Options," she said.

They walked back to Doug's apartment in silence. As soon as they closed the door, Casey began to cry. Doug did too. They hadn't planned on this. Casey was still bringing home straight A's. Doug had hoped he could travel some after graduation—walk across Europe with a couple of friends, maybe, or start his first book. But now, their future seemed broken even before it began. They felt scared: Scared for themselves, scared of what the baby might mean, scared about what kind of parents they'd be.

But above all that, they feared what their parents would say.

Through the tears, the two began to talk. Neither considered abortion an option: They couldn't just wipe away the problem. And Casey couldn't imagine giving up the child for adoption. Casey wanted to keep it, even though it meant talking with her mom and dad. The parents she loved as much as anyone in the world. The parents who until then thought she could do no wrong.

Doug smiled, squeezed her hand, and walked into his tiny kitchen. Casey heard him open a drawer. When he returned, he was carrying a tiny twist tie, made into a ring. He bent down on one knee and took her hand. "Will you marry me?" he said. Casey nodded furiously, smiling as she cried some more.

But with that decision made, they couldn't put off the hardest part of this incredibly hard day.

Casey pulled out her phone and called home.

"Hello?" her mother said on the other end.

"Mom?"

"Casey!" Her mother replied. "Hold on, let me get your father." Casey imagined her mother putting the receiver against her chest, close to her heart. She heard a muffled call. In a moment, she heard an extension pick up, and then her dad's voice.

"Hey!" he said. "What's up, honey?"

Casey closed her eyes and said a quick, wordless prayer. She swallowed hard and began.

"I've got something to tell you. Something hard."

She could almost hear her parents' breath catch in that momentary pause.

"Honey," Mom said, "what is it?"

"Mom," Casey said, the pitch of her voice rising as she began to cry yet again, "I'm going to have a baby."

Silence.

Then, "Oh, God." Her mother. Casey heard her crying softly through the phone, a sound she had heard just once before, when her grandfather died. And she heard on the other extension the ragged breath of her father, growing louder.

Finally, he spoke.

"We're so disappointed in you, Casey," he said. "We're so disappointed in you."

He hung up.

The Perils of Perfect Parenting

"In this world you will have trouble," Jesus told us (John 16:33). Funny that we don't really believe it, that trouble could *really* come into our own homes, our own families. Casey could be your daughter. Doug could be your son. Maybe they could even be you. Or me.

Focus on the Family, the organization I serve, is dedicated to helping prevent days like this from ever happening. On Focus's daily broadcast, I talk with some of the best, brightest minds about raising our kids. We've loaded our staff with pastors, counselors, and child-rearing experts. Our ministry is founded on giving parents practical, God-honoring advice on how to grow strong, loving families. And, God willing, this advice *works* most of the time. We all believe in Proverbs 22:6 (KJV): "Train up a child in the way he should go: and when he is old, he will not depart from it."

But there's a lot of wiggle room in that proverb, isn't there? The training doesn't always go smoothly. Kids can be frustratingly resistant to parents' lessons, and we're not always the best of teachers. And even when it seems like everything works, when we send our kids into the world on their own, confident we've trained them in the way they should go, things . . . happen. Unexpected things. Crushing things. None of us are perfect.

That very concept of perfection can be the biggest pitfall of all—and I think it's this pitfall that good Christian families tend to trip right into. Our desire to be perfect and to honor God through that perfection is actually destroying us.

Now, don't get me wrong. It's not bad to do our best. It's not bad to encourage our children to do the same. We want them to do well, and when they do, we should celebrate their successes, be it swimming across the pool for the first time, scoring the winning goal in soccer, or getting a hard-earned B in algebra.

But often, without our even noticing, we cross over that invisible line, from celebrating our kids' victories to accepting nothing less.

"A 'B'? It better be an A next time I check."

"Sure, maybe you scored a winning goal a week ago, but you sure whiffed on that pass tonight."

"Don't tell me you're afraid of the water. Stop crying! Get in there!"

And if our kids *actually* fail? If they *actually* make a mistake? Heaven help them. And if *you* make a mistake? If you fail your own kids somehow? Well, heaven help you too. You'll never forgive yourself.

And what happens if they succeed? What happens if and when kids reach our lofty expectations for them? Well, that opens up another litany of problems.

In his book *The Road to Character*, columnist and author David Brooks talks about how we tend to pursue two kinds of virtues: résumé virtues and what he calls "eulogy" virtues—the virtues people celebrate when we're gone.[1] And even though we know the superior value of those eulogy virtues, we teach our children to focus on the résumé virtues. We emphasize achievement, not character.

"So we've told a generation of kids how wonderful they are, and they believed us," Brooks told me in 2016. "And so, they think they have a little golden figure inside themselves that makes them intrinsically wonderful. And when you think that, then you don't have a sense of your own sinfulness, your own brokenness, and you can't build character, cause you think you're just wonderful."

And yet for all that confidence, these children are surprisingly vulnerable too—especially to the slings and arrows hurled at them by their own parents.

"I see an epidemic of conditional love in our culture," Brooks says. "Parents love their children, but they also really want them to succeed. And if the kids do something the parents think will lead to success, the beam of love beams stronger. And if they do something the parents think will not lead to success, the beam of love is withdrawn.

"And see, the most important relationship in those kids' lives is fragile," he adds. "They feel they have to earn it, and that destroys their inner criteria. It makes them terrified."

When our love feels conditional to our children, especially when it feels like they can't meet those conditions, it pushes them in one direction: away.

We've all heard the whole "pastor's daughter" cliché. The "PK" stereotype. Why do we always assume the pastor's daughter is going to be wild, or that the preacher's son is going to be the most frustrating kid in Sunday school? Why does it seem so predictable? I think it's because of the pressure of perfectionism and those unattainable expectations. Pastors can feel incredible pressure to be role models for their congregations, to walk the walk and not be hypocritical. That pressure trickles down, or gushes down, to the pastor's wife and children. Congregants may feel that, given the pastor's close walk with God, he and his family should be highly in tune with God's wishes. The pastor and his family should be, well, nearly perfect. Even if no one in the congregation ever asked him or expected him to be perfect, the pastor can feel that pressure himself.

We can talk until our faces turn blue about moderate, healthy expectations. Most of us think those *are* our expectations. But how do we deal with the failures, whether our own or those of our kids? What happens when we fail to achieve even our "modest" targets? How do we react then?

Feeling Failure

Not too long ago, a friend of mine—a man deeply involved in a prominent Christian ministry—came home from work to find his wife standing in the driveway, her eyes swollen from crying, her cheeks tracked with tears. He thought his mother-in-law must've died.

He got out of the car, took his wife into his arms, and asked, "What's wrong?"

"Nathan was looking at pornography," she said.

My friend said nothing. But inside, the news sent him reeling. Denial came first. Then confusion. Anger. Grief. A new understanding of our imperfections. *What should I say?* he wondered. *What do I need to do?* It all cascaded over him in the space of a heartbeat, but before he could say anything, Kathy poured out her own grief and anger.

"We've been terrible parents," she said. "How could we let this happen to our fourteen-year-old son?" She looked up at him. "How could *you* let this happen?"

That's what failure can look like. When someone in the family fails, it can feel like everyone fails—like everyone deserves punishment. When your children look at pornography, it can feel like a bomb just went off. BOOM.

But guess what? Similar bombs go off in American households every day. Every *minute*, probably. And it doesn't matter whether Bible verses hang on your refrigerator.

A University of New Hampshire study found that 62 percent of girls and a whopping 93 percent of boys had been exposed to pornography before they turned eighteen.[2] And these days, porn is just a click or two away. When I was growing up, boys might sneak a peek at a *Playboy* magazine when they were thirteen. Now, thanks to the Internet, kids are viewing porn at younger and younger ages. Our own resources at Focus on the Family say that the average age of first exposure is now eight years old. *Eight.* Some kids don't know how to ride a bike at that age.

Nathan's family knew the dangers. It wasn't as if they bookmarked the adult site to make it easier for Nathan to find. They took most of the steps they should've taken. They kept the computer in a public, well-used area of the house, not in Nathan's bedroom. Nathan's parents had installed tracking software to keep track of their kids' Internet habits. They'd talked with Nathan about the dangers of pornography.

But accidents can happen. Parents can get complacent. And children can be pretty sneaky. If a weakness or a loophole exists somewhere, they'll probably find it.

In this case, the company that had made the tracking software had gone under, so the software had stopped functioning. And so when Kathy installed some new tracking software on the family PC, it ratted Nathan out. Every inappropriate site that Nathan had visited in the last six months got revealed for the world—well, at least all the world that mattered to Nathan—to see.

I don't want to minimize this. Porn is bad, obviously. No Christian parent wants their teen boy looking at dirty pictures. They're demeaning and exploitative and can seriously twist our notions of sex into something damaging.

So who failed here? And what was the level of failure?

Maybe Mom and Dad could've done more with their tracking software or had more heart-to-hearts with Nathan. But they didn't type in Nathan's inappropriate searches for him. They hadn't pressed the button. Nathan pressed the button. He typed the searches. He did what 93 percent of boys had done. He's the one at fault. But did that make him a failure?

When I played quarterback for Yucca Valley High School in Southern California, I learned that success meant more than making the right throws: I had to have a short memory when I made the wrong ones. You learn from your mistakes, but you have to shake them off too. You have to keep throwing. You can't be afraid. You can't hang your head in shame. Not if you want to win.

I think there's a lesson here for Christian families, even though it's a hard one for us to learn. When we make a mistake, we should shake it off. We keep throwing. We may fail, but that doesn't mean we're failures.

Not Good Enough

A long, terrible night unfolded at Nathan's house that evening.

Kathy blamed her husband. She blamed Nathan. She blamed herself. It felt like the walls of her world had fallen in.

But as much as she felt hurt, Nathan might've been hurting more. He punished himself more than his parents ever could.

For most of that evening, Nathan sat in the darkness in his room, feeling disgusted and ashamed. And that night, he handed his parents a letter.

"I've broken my trust with you," it said. "It's going to take time to earn that trust back."

He apologized for what he'd done and said he'd do his best to make it up, even though he knew it would take time. And then he said, "I've broken God's heart. I've lied to Him."

His awesome letter was humble, contrite, and submissive in the healthiest of ways. Nathan made a mistake and was trying to make up for it the best way he knew how.

He signed it, "Not good enough."

Not good enough.

Don't we all struggle with that in our families? All of us—moms and dads, parents and kids—feel we're not good enough. We fear we'll *never* be good enough. We brand ourselves with our failures and always carry the scars.

We have such high expectations for our children. We want them to excel and achieve, be stars in the classroom or on the football field or on stage. We want them to be respectful and kind (but not be a pushover), to be honest (but not to a fault), to be strong and sweet and independent and obedient.

I've put that sort of pressure on my own kids. I've caught myself when my own sons, Trent and Troy, come home with a grade below their effort level.

"Do you guys want to be ditchdiggers?" I've been known to say. I'm embarrassed I've said that.

Once Trent turned the tables on me. "What's wrong with being a ditchdigger if I'm loving the Lord?" he said. I still want Trent to work hard and do the best he can in school, but it gave me something to think about. *OK, so I'm a ditchdigger*, he was saying. *I love God, Dad. Isn't that OK? Isn't that enough for you?*

Sometimes I think we want our kids to be better than we are. To make up for our own mistakes. And when they fall short of who we want and expect them to be, both parents and kids feel the failure.

Not good enough.

When our children suffer, we all feel the pain. When our children fail, we feel we're to blame. *If only we had said the right thing on Monday. If only we'd kept quiet on Tuesday. We shouldn't have pushed so hard. We didn't push hard enough.*

And if we're Christians, we can be especially hard on ourselves. We want to show the world that Jesus makes *everything* better. We feel the pressure to be better parents. Our children feel the pressure to be better kids. Heaven help us if our kid says the wrong thing in church! And the help of heaven might not feel like enough if you're the pastor.

I think as Christian parents, too many of us are driving our kids to be stars. To be the doctor, be the honor roll kid, achieve all these outward attributes of success. And the sad thing is that when Christians feel so much pressure to be the perfect Christian family, we sometimes force our kids to run the other way.

When many Christian young people leave home, they also leave their religion. Millennials—young adults between the ages of eighteen and thirty-four—are far more likely to be religiously unaffiliated than their parents or grandparents, according to a study from Pew Research. A full 36 percent of younger millennials say they're religiously unaffiliated.[3] And this trend isn't showing any signs of slowing down: the younger you are, the more likely you are to believe in *nothing*.

But I don't think youth and young adults are walking away from God so much as they're walking away from control and parental authoritarianism. They're leaving those suffocating expectations their well-meaning parents have saddled them with and running as far in the other direction as they can.

Not long ago, I heard the story of a woman who thought she'd fostered the perfect Christian environment in which to raise her daughter. She married a pastor and followed all the rules. Then she sent her daughter off to college and didn't see her again for a year.

Then one day while on Facebook, the woman came across a picture of a girl she pitied. Stringy hair fell into the skinny girl's eyes, her arms and chest covered with tattoos. The woman felt sure something had to be seriously wrong with her. Either she had an eating disorder or was on drugs. *That poor girl*, she thought.

Then she looked at the picture a little closer and slowly recognized her own daughter.

So many people in the Christian community are so concerned with appearance, with the impression they want to leave on the outside world. They're all about the letter grade—the A's and B's. We don't want anyone to think we're struggling. We don't want anyone to think we're ditchdiggers. And so we neglect the condition of our own hearts. We've somehow convinced ourselves that how we present ourselves outwardly, how close we can appear to approach perfection, is far more important than what's really going on.

That's pretty rich, considering that Jesus taught us exactly the opposite.

Finding Hope in Heartache

Remember Casey and Doug, the couple at the beginning of the chapter? Let me tell you something about them. They're doing just fine.

They've been married for twenty-five years now. Their baby—the one that sent their lives careening in a different direction—recently graduated from college. Casey's parents came alongside and gave them all the emotional support they could. They all still live in the same town, and the whole family still gathers around the family dining room table every week or so.

Casey originally thought of her unexpected pregnancy as God's judgment, a punishment. "And maybe it was," she says. "But it was also a blessing. The greatest blessing I can imagine."

No matter how hard you try, you won't transform into a flawless mom or dad. You won't find anywhere a foolproof Top Ten list of how to create the ideal family—and certainly not here. After talking with hundreds of family experts, leading Focus on the Family for years, and being a father myself, I know there's no such thing.

But I do want to point you in a different direction, a path away from self-conscious perfectionism, which can lead you, I hope, to a place of comfort and love and a sense of home. It's a place where milk gets spilled and glasses fall to the floor, where both kids and parents make mistakes. But in the middle of the chaos and mess, there's love. There's forgiveness. There's grace.

You might not be perfect by the time you reach the end of this book. I know I won't be in writing it! But maybe we'll shake that sense of inferiority most of us carry, the crippling idea that we're not good enough. And when we get to that point, that's where great families can begin.

Chapter Two

WHAT A FAMILY IS

✦

S o, what is a good family?

We overcomplicate the question. We know what a good family looks like. Kids feel safe. Communication is easy and free. Love is always present, even when kids get punished or moms and dads fight. I didn't grow up in a great family, but I knew what one looked like.

I learned about fatherhood by what I was missing from my own fathers. My absent bio dad and my stepfather, who abandoned me after my mom's funeral when I was nine. I learned about motherhood from the all-too-brief example my own mom gave me. I know what a good family can mean to a kid because of what it would've meant to me, had I had one. And my love of family, along with my desire to see that others didn't miss out like I did, eventually led me to Focus on the Family, an organization that has been telling men and women about God's design for families for nearly forty years.

In 2014, we took much of our ministry's collective wisdom—the knowledge of scores of scholars and experts and the opinions of everyday people—and distilled it into something we call "The Family Project." Throughout the project's twelve-session journey, we hear why strong families are so paramount not just for our kids but for our culture as well. It's as good a place as any to dive in earnest into our discussion.

"Family is the force that defines society," Rabbi Shmuel Goldin says in The Family Project. "Society should not mold the family; family should mold the society."[1]

Some, of course, will disagree. They'll tell you that families, at least traditional families, aren't all that important. *Who cares?* they'll say. *Everybody's coming from crappy families anyway.* Some might even point to my own background as proof. *Hey, Jim Daly didn't have a great family, and he turned out OK.* Many people now say there really is no such thing as a traditional family. Our concepts of what a family is or should be are radically outdated or perhaps never existed anywhere except in our own minds.

There's some truth in that. Families do indeed come in many forms. Loving families need not be wholly traditional. Traditional families are not always that loving. I came from a broken, flawed, totally messed-up family—and yet, thanks to a few key elements, my brothers, sisters, and I actually turned out all right.

I believe that family, when done right, is the building block of our culture. Even more important, it reflects God's own love for us.

My wife, Jean, really helped me see this reflection in our own home. We have two boys, Trent and Troy. And like brothers everywhere, they can emotionally poke each other like you might a sleeping dog, just to see if it'll growl.

But whenever the boys pick on each other, Jean swoops in. "Hey, we're a family," she'll say. "Family is a safe place. Family is where we should have love for each other and have confidence in ourselves and be just whoever we are. Be the real us—and be loved."

I think that's exactly the kind of vulnerability the Lord wants from us. As part of His family, I can be the real me, the sinful me, and still be loved.

Think about how moms and dads love their children—an unyielding, unconditional love. It'd be nearly impossible for kids to strain or break that love, no matter what they do. Isn't that how our heavenly Father thinks about us? That "neither death nor life, neither angels nor demons, neither the present nor the future, nor any powers, neither height nor depth, nor anything else in all creation, will be able to separate us from the love of God" (Romans 8:38–39)? What can we do to separate us from His love? Absolutely nothing! A parent's love for his or her child is a reflection of God's love for us. The concept of family is, at least in part, God trying to tell us how much we mean to Him.

The Traditional Family

I believe the ideal family is made up of three main parts: a mom, a dad, and some kids.

This doesn't mean the only way to have a loving, safe family is in a traditional two-parent household. I'm proof that things can turn out OK even without it. But the statistics tell us that it's harder to achieve, and most single parents would say the same thing. Parenting really is a two-person job, and it's part of God's design. Biology requires two people to start a family: the woman supplies the egg; the man supplies the sperm. And I believe that God means for us to stick together past that moment of conception. Our whole biology encourages it.

From a family's inception, our divine design works to tie us close together. When we hug or kiss someone, scientists tell us that our brains release something called oxytocin, sometimes called a "bonding hormone," which helps create a stronger sense of intimacy and kinship with the person we're touching. A lot of oxytocin gets stirred up in sex, which naturally helps to more closely bind sexual partners together. We're biologically and chemically predisposed to gather in traditional families—husbands and wives, parents and kids. Physical touch and intimacy makes us ever more prone to be emotionally intimate with one another.

As a family moves forward in that design, we learn to appreciate not only the things that pull us ever closer together, like the physical contact and the love, but even the things you might think would drive us apart. Even our differences can work to unite us.

That perfectly describes what happens with my wife and me. Jean is more of a science-loving introvert; I'm more of the marketing extrovert. And while our differences can generate unique challenges, both in our marriage and in our parenting (which you'll hear more about later), God brought us together for a reason. Together, we're stronger because we complement each other.

Both of us, of course, can be loving, effective parents without the other. We both manage just fine when the other is gone. But together, we hit a sweet spot. Jean's rational decision making and desire for the whole family to do its best, combined with my go-with-the-flow, relish-the-mess style, make for some tricky moments of give-and-take. But when we deal with our kids, whether praising them, disciplining them, or just hanging out with them, it allows us to give them, we hope, just what they need in that moment. Without question, we're better together.

Mother: The Foundation

If one gear in the average family makes the whole thing work, it's most likely Mom. Moms are predictable, dependable, stable. She's the first face to smile at us when we're born, and she's often the last face we see when we're tucked in at night. She'll kiss our skinned knees, cook us chicken noodle soup when we're sick, and help us with our homework (but never do it for us). Mama polar bears fast for eight months while they feed their cubs in their dens; mama orangutans never lose physical touch with their babies for four months. But when it comes to love and a willingness to give, nothing in the animal kingdom holds a candle to what our moms do for us. When Rasmussen Reports polled women about the importance of mothers, six out of ten of them said that motherhood was the most important role that women fill.[2] There's a reason that athletes or people in a crowd always seem to say, "Hi, Mom," when they're staring into a camera. There's a reason that Americans spend nearly $20 billion every Mother's Day.

In many ways, moms make us who we are, for better or worse. Studies suggest that moms have more influence on us than anyone else, and their influence is particularly strong when we're young and our brains are still incredibly pliable. They help determine what we think is right or wrong, healthy or unhealthy. They praise us when we're good, scold us when we're bad, and give us our first and most enduring understanding of what a "good person" looks like. And even when we're no longer holding their hands to cross the street, mothers still, in many respects, point the way forward.

"The mother's love for her child is probably the most powerful love that one human being has for another. There's something about that love," author Eric Metaxas said in The Family Project. "The umbilical cord, metaphorically, can never be cut."[3]

Kids who never connect with their mothers end up with pretty sad results. According to Christian psychologist and author Dr. John Townsend, people who don't get the love and attention they need from their moms early on tend to struggle in relationships for the rest of their lives. "There's just no way to overestimate how important moms are," he says in The Family Project.[4]

Just how important are mothers? Even the Bible sees their influence as practically unmatched. Just look at Proverbs 31:25–29 (ESV):

> Strength and dignity are her clothing,
> and she laughs at the time to come.
> She opens her mouth with wisdom,
> and the teaching of kindness is on her tongue.
> She looks well to the ways of her household
> and does not eat the bread of idleness.
> Her children rise up and call her blessed;
> her husband also, and he praises her:
> "Many women have done excellently,
> but you surpass them all."

My mother died when I was nine. Even before her death, she wasn't around as often as I would have liked. No, she wasn't perfect.

She drank quite a bit before my birth. She never took us to church. And yet, even though we had very little time together, I still consider her the biggest single influence in my life.

The importance of moms in the family equation often prompts us to overlook the dad. And yet science shows that fathers also have a critical role in raising healthy kids.

Father: The Wild Card

When I wrote *The Good Dad*, I called many fathers the wild cards of the family. You could count on moms. You knew they'd be there. Dads, however, aren't always so dependable. I knew that from personal experience. Fathers desert their families more often than mothers, and today it seems more fathers than ever go their own way. When I was a kid, a family without a father seemed like a rarity. Most of my friends lived with their dads back in 1970. In 2010, only about 60 percent of kids had that same opportunity. About 15 million children today live without a dad, as I did. Lots of kids never even *meet* their fathers.

Even when dads find their way into the family picture, they sometimes lurk around the edges. Too busy with work. Too engaged with their pals. Too apt to hide in the garage or the basement.

But when dads get involved, it can mean the world to their kids.

Children with stable, involved fathers are "better off on almost every cognitive, social and emotional measure," according to the National Fatherhood Initiative.[5] These children are more ready to begin school and more likely to do well once there. They're less likely to engage in risky behaviors, to bully, or to get in trouble at school. Families with dads at home tend to be more economically stable. Girls with dads at home are less likely to become sexually active at a young age. The bond between dad and daughter impacts mightily her future relationships too. "Every boy or man she meets will automatically be measured against her dad, and that relationship," writes Carey Casey, CEO for the National Center for Fathering. "He is her ultimate standard and role model for manhood."[6]

When you look at how most two-parent families operate, you find that the mother is the dominant force during a child's first years. She cares for them and nurtures them close to home.

But the older kids get, the more their fathers take a bigger role in their lives. They tend to be a little tougher, push their children a little more, and force them to look ahead. Moms are a little like boat builders, hammering together seaworthy vessels that'll keep their kids safe and dry as they go through life. Dads hoist the sail. We help our kids catch the wind, teach them how to use it, and, at the right time, help them sail away.

"God has called fathers to lead his children into the future," Dr. Tony Evans says in The Family Project. "To lead them there in a responsible, well-disciplined way, where they have the values of the kingdom of God operating in their lives."[7]

Statistically, if you want children to be healthy and stable, give them a loving, caring mother. If you want children to succeed, give them a loving and engaged father. That doesn't mean a child won't succeed without a father or a child will be an emotional wreck without a mother. But when they work together, using their own God-given skills and abilities, they give their child a great foundation on which to build their lives.

Child: The Reason

Some would say all you need to have a family is a man and a woman. A growing number of couples skip the kids all together in order to concentrate on careers, travel, and each other. And sometimes, when these couples need something more in their lives, they get a dog or a cat. Maybe a goldfish.

I think these couples are missing out.

Sure, some people will brandish studies that suggest childless couples feel happier. They'll point out that it costs upward of $250,000 to raise a child to age eighteen (not counting the cost of this book). But they don't understand the joy in raising children that goes beyond superficial happiness. A value in watching them grow exceeds what we might otherwise amass in our bank accounts. Yes, parenting is hard and stressful and exasperating. But how many parents would trade their kids for a little peace and quiet? A nice vacation in Aruba? Not many.

I think children can make us better people too. They're so needy, which forces us to think of them before ourselves. They're so demanding, which makes us consider limits, both on them and us. They teach us patience. Self-control. The art of forgiveness. The beauty of unconditional love.

Or at least that's how it's supposed to work. I think that's how God *designed* it to work.

Unfortunately, our children don't always bring out the best in us. Sometimes they bring out the perfectionist in us. And that's a problem.

The Lie of the Ideal

If you bought this book hoping to find the last critical tool you need to build a perfect, ideal family, let me say a couple of words: forget it.

Although the family in some ways mirrors God's love for us, that doesn't mean it can (or even should) mirror His *perfection*. None of us are perfect. We're not without sin as people, and we're certainly not without fault as parents. I know I'm not. Even with those twin cornerstones of mother and father, the families we build look a little . . . weird. *All* of them. And many families make do without one cornerstone or another. Maybe Dad has left the picture. Maybe Mom has. Maybe Grandma and Grandpa are raising their second set of kids. Families come in many shapes and sizes, but they never come perfect.

God knows our flaws and circumstances better than anyone. God doesn't expect perfection from our families. And neither should we.

When I was a kid, if you were to ask me what a good family looked like, I'd point to the Bradys or Douglases on TV. I wouldn't point to mine. But my examples of good families weren't, in the end, *real* families. Call them aspirational myths, built around ratings, sponsorships, and a shared, collective ideal of what a family should look like. My family sure didn't look like *The Brady Bunch*. And you know what? Even if you grew up in a wonderful family with a loving mom and dad, I bet your home didn't look like that of the Bradys all the time either.

I wonder—do many of us have equally idyllic (and ultimately unrealistic) notions of what a family should look like?

In 2013, a study from the University of Michigan found that frequent users of Facebook generally felt less satisfied with their lives.[8] Researchers suspected that these Facebook users looked at all the smiling faces in their newsfeeds, like moms and dads and kids playing on vacation or celebrating a fifth-grade graduation ceremony, and judged their own lives less fulfilling by comparison. Some people now call Facebook Fantasybook.

I think that can happen with us when it comes to family. You don't need to be a kid from a broken home watching *The Brady Bunch* to feel a little familial envy. I know the Bradys pictured a blended family, but to many Americans, they were still the perfect family, led by a loving mother and father. They even had a clever housekeeper to liven things up. The point is, while none of us have perfect families, sometimes it seems like everyone else does. After all, we meet them in church. We hear about them at work. We see them in television commercials.

We even hang up their pictures in Focus on the Family's main entryway. Laughing children, caring parents, and sage grandparents all silently tell visitors what a healthy family *should* look like. And those of us who don't have perfect families? Sometimes we wonder where we went wrong.

I have happy pictures like that too—photographs of me and my wife, Jean, laughing and playing with our two wonderful boys, Trent and Troy. Those pictures show us at our best, our happiest, and our most idyllic, photos that wouldn't look out of place in Focus on the Family's greeting area.

But they don't tell the whole story.

I don't take pictures of the kids when they bring home a bad grade from school. Jean and I don't grab the camera when we're fighting. I don't pose for a selfie when I lose my patience—and I doubt I'm unusual. Few of us document those less-than-perfect moments. Certainly we don't frame them or stick them on our Facebook wall.

Believe me, the pictures in our greeting area may look perfect, but you won't see a perfect family represented on that greeting wall. All those smiling kids lie to their parents or talk back to authorities—and if they haven't yet, they will. Each parent pictured probably snaps at their kids when they'd be better off sitting back and listening. No such thing as a perfect family exists. And if it did, I'm certainly not the guy to write about it.

I know authors and "experts" who imply they have perfect families. They tell their readers or proclaim to their audiences that they know the secrets to making your family perfect too. *Spend an hour at the dinner table every day. Limit screen time. Hug your children at least four times daily. Don't be afraid of discipline.* None of these "secrets" are bad. Most of them can help. But do they guarantee anything? Nope. And ironically, even with these secrets in tow, the families of some of these leaders are in shambles. These authors, ministers, and parenting experts want so desperately to meet their audience's expectations, to show the world that they know how to do *family*, that they never see the true shape of their own families. Their friends may see the dysfunction, but the experts themselves remain blind to it.

The *ideal* of a perfect family, to live up to the pictures we see and sometimes take, has its place. We should set a goal, even if we'll never realistically reach it, just as we should all strive to be the persons God designed us to be, even if we'll never turn into that person here on earth. But the *idol* of a perfect family is something else. It's dangerous. A perfectionist streak sometimes weaves through our DNA. We make the mistake of believing, even subconsciously, that perfection is achievable. I believe that dads, especially, back away from fatherhood because we can't ever, really, get it right. We have a hard time scoring nines and tens in the parenting game. And sometimes we tell ourselves that if we can't get that perfect or near-perfect score, we won't do it at all. We just quit.

I suspect this tendency toward perfectionism can become an especially big problem in Christian circles. Our families are the ultimate report card. We feel like we're graded (and sometimes we are) on how well behaved or gifted or holy our kids seem. Families can feel a tremendous amount of pressure to be perfect, or at least to appear to be so. If our kids slip up, we see it as an assessment of our parenting skills. If they fail at something, so do we.

And so we parents can grow desperate to find perfection. We'll buy dozens of books to get a little closer. We'll follow all the templates set out by parenting experts, the ones who say, "If you follow these 14 steps, your children are guaranteed to love God and honor their parents and probably become doctors."

But building a family isn't like building a house. Even if you follow the blueprint, it won't necessarily look just like the pictures. Parenting isn't engineering. It's not a science. It's chaotic and unpredictable and messy from the first day on. There are no guarantees. And there's certainly no perfection to be found.

Parenting is more art than science. It's not a chemical formula, where you add this and that and the other thing, and *voila!*—a perfect family. Parenthood is more like home cooking, where our different tastes and inclinations balance and blend with each other, and only experience and love can make the dish turn out great.

Yes, like in baking, we can follow directions, rules, and guidelines that can help us along the way. We can (and will) tell you some of them. By following a few critical steps, you can improve the environment in your home and increase the likelihood of raising a healthy child.

But baking is messy work too. You get your hands dirty. This line of work offers no guarantees, gives no promises. No set of rules will guide you all the way home. That's why we must forget about copying the wonderful families we think we know and instead find our own recipe.

Putting Aside Perfection

When I think of family, I think of words like *love, safety, encouragement, affirmation,* and *peace.* I think about what I want my family to look like. And sometimes, when Jean and I are on top of our game and our kids cooperate, it looks something like I think it should. It looks a lot like what God intended.

Most of the time, though, those words seem like more of a wish list than what we find in reality. Families feel chaotic. Fragmented. Dysfunctional. The parents we love and admire aren't always lovable or admirable, any more than our children act unfailingly polite and well behaved. Our families are flawed and fallen, like everything in this world. Nothing completely and perfectly reflects God's design, not even the most perfect family, and no amount of wishing or prayer can change that.

But just because we can't have perfect families *all the time* doesn't mean we can't create good ones. We may not always be picture-perfect, but we can foster healthy, happy homes full of love and affirmation, enough to take all of us through the inevitable rough spots. Kids aren't asking for us to be perfect; they're asking us to be *present*—to try, every day, to give them the love, attention, and encouragement they need.

That's step number one to creating the right environment at home: to be present with them and engaged in their lives. That doesn't mean you necessarily need to be a stay-at-home parent (though it sure doesn't hurt) or sacrifice your own life and interests for the sake of your children (which can be counterproductive). But you do need to set a good tempo for your family, to show your sons and daughters that you love them, care about them, and will always be there for them when they need you.

We're not perfect! We can't be. But we have hope. With each day, we can get better at this family thing. With each mistake we make, we can learn something. And with each new lesson, we can crawl closer and closer, inch by inch, foot by foot, to becoming the parents God always wanted us to be.

Chapter Three

BROKEN OR REAL?

✦

Families are like cars—we climb into them at birth, and we count on them to carry us a long way down the road. But some run better than others, and you can't always tell their condition by how they look.

Growing up in Southern California, my early family probably would've looked to you like a 1985 Yugo, with the windows patched with duct tape and the muffler held up by fishing line. You might marvel that it ever ran at all.

If you've read some of my other books, you know just how close my family came to getting propped up on a set of cinder blocks. My natural father, an alcoholic, once came home drunk out of his skull, with a hammer in his hand, threatening to kill my mom. He died before my fourteenth birthday, found frozen in an abandoned building in Reno. My stepfather, Hank, was a hard, angry man who deserted me and my four brothers and sisters when we needed him most. By high school, I was pretty much on my own—but it felt, in many ways, like the adults in my life had abandoned me long before that. Our family looked broken, even totaled.

But when you look at the fruits of that family—me, my four brothers and sisters—we all seemed to turn out OK. Of course, we're not perfect. None of us are. We all carry scars. But overall we feel pretty healthy, even with all the trauma. And for that, I can thank the engine that made our family run—my mom.

Laughter Is the Best Medicine

We never had much money growing up. My mom worked crazy hours to feed us five kids, and it didn't always work. Some days we had no food, no milk, no bread, nothing. During some of those lean days, my mom would try to make our poverty seem like a game.

"Instead of milk, let's pour some Kool-Aid on your Cheerios!" she'd say. If I made a face, she'd counter by saying, "You like Kool-Aid, don't you?"

"Yeah."

"And you like Cheerios."

"Sure!"

"Well, they're *bound* to be great together, then!" she'd tell me, smiling. And whether it was her unflappable logic or her unquenchable enthusiasm, I smiled too.

I *didn't* like them, though. They tasted terrible. But it did put a little food in my six-year-old stomach, and she was trying her best.

But some days, not even the prospect of Kool-Aid or my mom's unflappable personality could cheer me up. Then she resorted to more drastic measures.

Around age six or seven, I fell into a serious funk, probably when I realized I was too young to run with my teenage siblings, who had no time for little brother. I felt lonely. So one afternoon, Mom and my older brother, Dave, brought home a flat, colorful cardboard box that read "Twister" on the top ("the game that ties you up in knots").

I don't know where she got the cash for it. But she brought it home, along with a number of other mysterious bags, and immediately popped open the box and suggested that Dave and I play it. She volunteered to spin the dial. "Good luck!" she told me.

Now, by then I'd barely learned to tie my shoes. Dave was probably fifteen or sixteen, much bigger and more coordinated than I was. He could reach those sprawling, colored polka dots far more easily than I could. If Vegas had offered wagers on our Twister game, I would have been the longest of long shots.

But somehow, in an upset for the ages, I won! In recognition of my amazing victory, Mom told me I'd earned a prize. Beaming, she handed me a package of underwear.

"See? Look what you won!" she said. "Do you want to play again?"

"Yeah!" I said, thrilled with my squishy first-place gift. "Let's do it again!"

And so Dave and I played Twister for what seemed like the whole afternoon. Strangely, I always won, and Mom—smiling and laughing all the while—seemed to have a prize for me after every victory. None of the prizes seemed particularly special in and of themselves: shirts, socks, things I needed anyway for school. But because I "won" them on an otherwise unremarkable afternoon, they became truly special to me, almost like birthday presents. The socks meant as much to me as if they had been bikes and baseball mitts.

But what really made the afternoon so memorable, so vivid, that even fifty years later I can still remember it like it happened last week, was how much fun we had. I think my mom loved to see me have such a good time after falling into such a miserable funk. And I loved to hear Mom laugh. Our mutual happiness fed off each other. In that moment, the fun we had was worth a week of Cheerios-and-Kool-Aid breakfasts.

Even today, knowing how many experts would criticize so much of this moment—experts who'd tell me that "good" parents don't fritter away hard-earned money on frivolous board games or that they shouldn't shield their children from the hard realities of Twister competitions—this still feels like an example of what my mom did well. She couldn't take away all our pain, so she helped us laugh our way through it.

Caring through Crisis

Mom was a ham. And her larger-than-life personality became the beating heart of our family.

She loved the theater. I remember when she took me to the play *My Fair Lady* in Pasadena, California, and escorted me backstage to meet the stars. My brothers and sisters tell me she spent a lot of time with the PTA. She'd write plays for the school and even sew the costumes. I don't know if as a little girl she ever dreamed of becoming an actress, whether she imagined lounging in a flower-filled Broadway dressing room with a star on the door (like I used to imagine being the quarterback for a pro football team). But it seems logical. Her life took her in a different direction, however, and so her kids became her adoring audience.

I have my most vivid memories of her when she was about fifty or so. But her maturity didn't stop her from turning her dentures upside down to get a laugh out of us. Even when she became a hardworking restaurant manager, she still wrapped her middle in a "diaper" made from a towel, popped a pacifier in her mouth, and danced around like a toddler. She'd do practically *anything* for a laugh. Maybe that's because we didn't have much to smile about otherwise.

My mom played the clown. But today I can see that she used her sense of humor more than to just make us laugh. We had a great time the afternoon we played Twister, laughing so hard that our sides hurt. But she wanted to do more than laugh or give me "prizes" or even create a treasured memory. She wanted to make me feel safe. Appreciated. Loved.

The memories I have of my mother are very precious to me, all the more so because I don't have a lot of them.

For several years—critical, formative years in my childhood between the ages of five and eight—she raised five kids on her own as a single mom. She worked as a waitress and a restaurant manager, which meant lots of evening and weekend work. Most weekdays, she'd get home by midnight (if she was lucky), and when I left for school, she was still sleeping. By the time I walked home around 3:00 p.m., Mom was backing the car down the driveway, heading to the restaurant.

I remember many days when I'd run to the car just as she was leaving, sprinting to the driver's side just to hug her. I'd hang on the door, as if I could somehow pull the car to a stop and keep her with me. She'd slowly drive just a foot or two with me hanging on the door, just for fun. We'd giggle over the shared joke. And then I'd beg her to bring me home a chocolate shake.

The next morning, I'd find a chocolate shake waiting for me in the refrigerator. I'd drink it for breakfast. Although it might've been worse for me than Cheerios and Kool-Aid, it fostered in me a love for chocolate shakes that I still have (healthy habit or not). Those shakes remind me of the special bond between me and my mom. Before she left her shift, I knew she'd be thinking of me. And as I slurped down that shake as she slept in the next room, I knew she loved me.

Those little things meant so much to me. They helped me endure some of the storms that came later. Whatever rocked my life, I always felt loved. I felt accepted. I believed she would always be there when I needed her.

Sometimes I saw her for only a few minutes a day, when I was coming home and she was leaving. That instant when I hung on the door, only halfway joking that I could somehow make her stay home. A tiny exchange, really. But somehow, it was enough.

I knew early on that life was hard, that our family wasn't perfect and never would be. But in a way, those very problems helped give my mom and her kids an ability to deal lightly with life and with all the heavy calamities that came with it. When problems hit, we could laugh about them. And if we couldn't laugh, at least we could shrug and find a way to move on.

I think that ability has become one of my strengths, both as a leader and as a father. Certainly I'm not perfect; I make plenty of mistakes. But I don't rattle easily. And when people say to me, "Problems just roll off you like water off a duck's back," I give credit to just two relationships in my life: the Lord and my mom. She earns the trophy for building that ability into me and into all of us Daly kids, in fact. I find it hard to believe she did that in just a few minutes a day. We learned from her that, even when life knocks you on your heels, you can't let the pain linger. You gotta shake it off.

Amazing, isn't it? My family looked broken, and in a lot of ways, it was. But despite that, and maybe because of it, we learned how to deal with our own brokenness and the splinters of brokenness around us. No one would ever mistake my mom for a picture-perfect mother. But she still managed to give her five kids the critical tools they needed to survive. She gave us the resiliency to push through our problems and the ability to laugh in the midst of them. She couldn't always feed us, but she gave us a different kind of security. We always knew we were loved and cared for.

Although our quirky, chaotic little family might've looked broken to the outside world, it got us where we needed to go.

At least for a while.

Shattered

In his book *Anna Karenina*, Leo Tolstoy wrote, "Happy families are all alike; every unhappy family is unhappy in its own way."[1] With all due respect to Tolstoy, I doubt that's true. While every family is indeed unique, the unhappy families that I've seen and even been a part of seem to "break" in only a handful of ways.

Dr. Tim Elmore, founder of the Growing Leaders ministry and a frequent guest on the Focus on the Family daily program, says our mistakes fall into one of two areas: *abundance* or *abandonment*. That seems right to me. As a child, I probably had more experience with the *abandonment* part of the equation—situations that to the outside world look especially broken. Addiction or abuse can tear apart families; one or both parents can let their anger make them inattentive.

But these days in my role at Focus, I've come to believe more of us suffer from the problem of *abundance*, and maybe especially Christian families. We hover too much. We lecture too often. We get so focused on our children's happiness and success that we never let them fail. We hone in so intently on our children's performance—and our own as parents—that we develop an unhealthy and wholly futile drive for perfection.

How strange that anyone should use the word *perfection* in conjunction with Christianity! Of all the world's big religions, only Christianity tells us explicitly that we *can't* achieve perfection. While Buddhists seek Nirvana and Jews seek to follow the Law, we Christians live under a blanket of grace. God knows how messed up we are, and yet God loves us even when we inevitably miss the mark.

But why, then, despite this divine shower of grace, do we struggle to show that same grace to our spouses and children? The world calls out us Christians for being judgmental, and way too often the world has a point. We in the Christian community continually speak the words "unconditional love" and "saved by grace," but we rarely apply them, whether in the culture at large or in our own homes. And so we mess up our relationships in horrible ways.

A few guys in Christian ministry talk incessantly about grace and forgiveness, but secretly (or in some cases, not so secretly) believe they've gotten over the whole "sin" thing. They've arrived at total sanctification. They've become exactly the person God wants them to be. But you know what? Their families, or at least the families I'm aware of, are utterly broken. The struggles of their grown children have led them to rebellion. Now, these leaders might say their families suffered because of the very ministries they led—the distractions, the interruptions, the demands, the fame. But I'm not so sure. I believe that when once you think you've arrived, spiritually speaking, you lose your humility. You lose your ability to engage with people who, inescapably, are so much "weaker."

And what happens when those weaker people are your very own children? You demand more from your kids than they can ever deliver, which leads to fights, resentment, rebellion, and estrangement. It's dangerous and utterly unhealthy to imagine you've arrived. We're all broken, and imagining ourselves as faultless only reveals the worst kind of vanity. On this earth we cannot arrive at a place where we no longer sin. If we could do that, we wouldn't need Jesus.

But even those of us who know we're broken and who know deep in our bones our desperate need for God's grace still feel tempted by the siren call of perfection. We don't want to show ourselves as anything less than perfect. We hate to show weakness of any sort. And because we feel we get judged as parents by how well our kids perform or behave, we can demand perfection, or near perfection, from them too.

Few, if any, parents would say they expect perfect kids. But sometimes our actions expose our good intentions as lies.

A dysfunctional family takes root when a parent begins to seed unhealthy behavior. It happens when moms and dads try to shame or demean their sons or daughters to teach them a lesson. It happens when they use insults or biting sarcasm to drive their point home. Eventually, it reaches the point where a child can feel as though he or she can never be good enough. And then what happens? The kids check out. They know they can never reach the bar. And so their behavior takes a nosedive, which ironically makes parents raise the bar even higher.

It doesn't take a genius to figure out what happens next. Kids want—no, they *need*—to feel love and acceptance. So they try to find that love and acceptance with friends. They know their friends will accept them, no matter what, even if they do drugs, have sex, or drink heavily. They know their friends will love them regardless. And maybe their circle of friends even encourages such behavior. Suddenly, the things that parents tried to shame their children into *not* doing become the very things that they think they *have* to do in order to feel loved. They get love the only way they know how—the love they should've gotten at home all along.

In the Christian community, we never stop talking about grace. We base our faith and our whole lives on it. Those of us in the evangelical world hear constantly that we can't work our way to heaven. But what happens when it comes to our kids? Sometimes we forget. And when we do, our unconditional love becomes *very* conditional, *very* performance driven. In our crusade to create perfect kids, we drive them away.

Breaking Bonds

In 2014, *Rolling Stone* magazine told the story of a young woman named Jackie, who was raised in a pious Christian home.[2] Her parents expected near perfection, and for most of her childhood, Jackie gave it to them.

"There was a standard to meet," Jackie told the magazine. "And I had met that standard my whole life. I was a straight-A student, the president of every club, I was in every sport. I remember my first day of college, my parents came with me to register for classes, and they sat down with my adviser and said, 'So, what's the best way to get her into law school?'"

But during her sophomore year at the University of Idaho, she called her mother to tell her she was gay. After a long pause, her mom finally responded. "I don't know what we could have done for God to have given us a f-g as a child," she said. The phone went dead. Soon, Jackie's debit card died too. Through Jackie's brother, her parents told her she'd need to return the car they had given her or they'd report it stolen.

According to *Rolling Stone*, Jackie's story is not unusual. The magazine suggests that it's a big reason that, even though gays and lesbians make up just 5 percent of the youth population, they account for 40 percent of the youth homeless population. When I talk with gay activists, they echo those statistics and suggest they might even be

worse. One activist told me that about 70 percent of the men he knows
in the gay movement come from conservative Christian homes—and
he's one of them. He said he never felt love and acceptance in his own
family, so he left to find it somewhere else.

I can't verify that 70 percent statistic. I can't say (and neither can
Rolling Stone) just how many Christian parents ostracize their gay
youth. But even if it hovers near the truth, shouldn't we Christians
study this more? Could children who feel inadequate at home, who feel
as if they can't meet their father's or mother's expectations, find those
familial pressures so severe that it could impact even the core of their
sexual orientation? Could that, along with many other contributing
factors, lead a child into same-sex attraction? I'd like to know what
researchers might say.

If we love our kids and want to be a positive influence in their
lives, shouldn't we do what we can to preserve our relationships with
them, even when they turn their backs on our values? When they scrap
the dreams we've had for them? Parents are the biggest influencers
in their children's lives, even as those children head into adulthood.
What we believe *matters* to them. But when we convey to them, by
abandoning or ostracizing them, that they don't matter to *us* anymore,
our influence stops. As soon as we cut off that love line to them, we
cut off our ability to speak into their lives. How can we presume to tell
them what we believe and why we believe it when we also give them
the impression that if they don't believe likewise, they're on their own?

I think a lot of homes and families have broken or are breaking
because the kids discover their parents' "unconditional" love had
conditions after all. Instead of creating a loving home, parents sometimes craft a dysfunctional environment where children receive regular
performance reviews. If they perform well, they get promoted in the
family hierarchy, showered with praise and perks. If they don't, we let
them know. We raise the bar. We scold. We shout. We punish, not so
much in the hopes that the punishment will change the behavior, but
because the child has been bad. He *deserves* it. The child gets a label

pasted on him—the bad kid, the problem child, the good-for-nothing. And once you start labeling a kid, he often starts living the label.

On the outside, these kinds of families may seem OK—for a while. Like an exotic sports car parked in the driveway that hides a blown engine, these families can *look* pretty great. But inside the family, its members know something is wrong. Broken. We can create a stench in our families. Our families can overflow with unhealthy control, unhealthy anger.

Would you say you're there most days? Then something's not healthy. Something's broken. And you have to find a way to remedy it *right now*. If you haven't done the work of creating a loving, joyful, humorous home environment, no eighteen- or nineteen-year-old will want to come back after they leave.

Making Contact

I played Little League baseball as a boy. One afternoon, as I waited for my own game to start, I watched another game in process.

Sometime in the seventh inning, near the end of the game, the batting, trailing team had loaded the bases for the next batter—a small, skinny boy about my age. You could tell from his face he would rather have been anywhere but at the plate.

Now, you might think that one baseball game is no big deal, that it's "just a game," a dime a dozen. You don't put the box scores on a college transcript or include them on your résumé. The seventh game of the World Series it is not. Still, anyone involved in youth sports knows that each game, each at bat, can feel hugely important to the kids who are playing. And sometimes the parents take it more seriously than the kids do.

This boy made that sad discovery.

The fired-up parents shouted and jeered in the stands. Just a few minutes earlier, a couple of them had gotten into a fight over a call—nasty words, fists, the whole bit. Tensions already ran pretty high. Kids in the dugout yelled, kids in the outfield heckled, while parents screamed. It all created a pressure-packed moment.

Too pressure packed, it turned out.

The batter felt so scared and stressed that he literally wet his pants, right there at home plate. I could see the wet spot spread across his gray britches. He couldn't hide. He wet his pants, and the whole world—at least *his* world—saw.

I wonder—could some of those screaming parents have been *his* parents? Probably. Could the pressure he felt from his *own* family have helped create what happened that afternoon? And how did his mom and dad respond afterward?

During a radio broadcast in 2010, I told that story to Dr. Tim Kimmel, who cofounded the Family Matters ministry with his wife, Darcy. He knows what he would've done had he been the boy's dad: "I would hope I would just walk right on out there to him, just pick him up in my arms, and say, 'Don't worry about this, son. I love you. We're gonna get beyond this thing,'" he told me. "I think when it comes to raising my kids, the mantra we've always used is treat your kids the way God treats his kids. And what would God do to you if you had one of those embarrassing moments? Would he just say, 'Get over it, for crying out loud. Cowboy up here!'? No. He wraps his arms around us. He cares about us."

The batter struck out. What else? He had to walk back to the dugout, back to his team, his pants soaking wet. He looked utterly alone.

That could've been me. It could've been any of us. In fact, all of us probably have had moments like that, where we felt thoroughly shamed. Embarrassed. We felt like total failures. None of us like to feel vulnerable or weak. But we do feel that way sometimes because we *are* vulnerable and weak.

In times like those, the Lord can most effectively meet us. That vulnerability is exactly what He wants from us. He approves of raw honesty. God sees the worst in us, the real us, the sinful us. And He still loves us.

My mom did that so effectively with me and the rest of us Daly kids. Despite our chaotic world, despite its brokenness and failure, we never doubted her love for us. She scolded us sometimes. She corrected us. But none of us ever doubted her love for us.

And then she was taken away from us.

Put to the Test

Doctors diagnosed my mom with colon cancer when I was nine years old. We lived in Long Beach, California, at the time. She and Hank—my angry, unbending stepfather—hadn't been married very long. Dreams of their shared lives took a tragic detour. He grew angrier and more frustrated, burdened with four children (my oldest brother, Mike, by then had joined the Navy) he never wanted and never imagined he'd need to raise by himself. Sometimes at the dinner table, when he'd try to pray, he'd shake with sobs as we kids snickered at him under our collective breath.

In a way, I lost my mother before she ever died. Hank shut her off, literally locking her away in their bedroom and taking charge of the key. Maybe it's because he knew what kind of mom my mom was. He could probably see that she would give herself to us, despite her illness. Maybe he worried that she'd pour every ounce of herself into her kids—every smile, every laugh, every shred of energy she had left. *She needed that energy for herself,* he might've thought. She needed all of her strength to fight her cancer. She couldn't use it on us.

When I think about it in that context, I can't feel too upset with Hank. He probably thought he was doing the right thing. But it doesn't make the downside for us any less painful. By locking her away, he took away the last bit of time my mom and I could've spent together.

I didn't see my mother for weeks. To make matters worse, I didn't even know she was dying. I couldn't distinguish between a common cold and terminal cancer, and nobody was telling anything to the baby in the family.

I have only one memory of seeing her during that dark time.

I came home one day and saw the bedroom door open. I knew Hank would be furious that he hadn't locked the door before he left, and I knew he'd be furious with me if I went in. So when I walked through the door, I hesitated. But Mom called out to me and beckoned for me to come closer.

I've told this story before, how it shocked me to see how different she looked, how her short auburn hair now framed her thin, gaunt face. But the same smile lit up her face! She flashed that same smile she had when she served me Kool-Aid and Cheerios, when I hung on her car door, when she spun that Twister dial. That smile told me, without a word, *You are my little boy. My light. My treasure.*

Her smile patched the brokenness one more time, before she would break from this world for good.

She died not long after our last visit. When she died, it felt like my world ended. In many ways, she *was* my world. She was my example, my energy. She was the only love I knew.

And yet I lived on. Her dying, and even her death, didn't crush me. And I owe that to her as well.

I didn't spend those days curled up next to my mother's closed door. I found different ways to live. I enjoyed school and did well in it. I played outside, running around, riding my bike, doing experiments in the garage, blasting off bottle caps in the driveway, finding turtles and snakes in the yard. All the normal things little boys do. I was growing into my own skin. I loved my mom, but the skills she taught me enabled me to live without her.

Although we spent so little time together, in those moments, somehow, she gave me such a foundation of love and acceptance, resilience, and self-assurance that I could weather even her death. It's kind of weird to think about. It's as though she found a way to release me as a nine-year-old, and I was ready to roll.

I wish I could turn to my mom today and tell her what she meant to me. What she taught me. How much I loved her—and still do. And someday, I trust I'll be able to see her again. But for now, let me tell you what she taught me: A healthy family isn't about following all the right rules, doling out the perfect punishment, or raising straight-A students to be doctors or lawyers or ministry leaders; it's about giving your children the ability to deal with adversity. To roll with the punches. To laugh. To cry and not feel ashamed.

Digging Deep

That last afternoon with Mom, she asked me to do something for her. She wanted me to go to the store, buy a packet of chrysanthemum seeds, and plant them right outside her window.

She never had the chance to smell those flowers. Nor did I. Hank sold the house and left the day after my mom's funeral. But watching the chrysanthemums bloom was beside the point, and I think Mom knew it. In asking me to perform this last favor for her, she allowed me to create one last memory of her—to feel the dirt crumble in my hands, to smell its sweet, fresh, loamy scent. In asking me for this small gift, Mom continued to give.

Families are not only like cars; they're also like gardens. They can be messy, dirty places filled with weeds and bugs, too much water, too much sun. They require work and patience and often a willingness to get knee-deep in mud. It also helps to have a sense of humor as you tend to them.

But gardening is also an act of trust. An act of faith. Underneath the earth, a miracle grows—one that has less to do with you and more to do with God. You can't *make* a seed sprout. You can't *force* it to flower. Your job is to help the miracle along.

PART TWO

✦

Building a
Better Family

Chapter Four

THE FUNDAMENTALS

✦

Weʼve established that perfection is the enemy of parenting. We know that the key to developing a good home life isnʼt pushing your kids to get all Aʼs or asking them to habitually knock in the winning run. We need to take our cues from Jesus. Just as grace is critical in our spiritual life, so it is in our family life. We need to be ready to show this grace to our kids, to our spouses, and even to ourselves. We need to push away the concept of mistake-free families and wrap our arms around a messier way of doing things. And we need to understand that even when we donʼt do everything right, we can help grow loving, virtuous, successful children.

But before you start cracking out the Kool-Aid and Cheerios, letʼs take a step back. Iʼm advocating *imperfect* parenting, not *indifferent* parenting. We shouldnʼt slavishly focus on the rules of the parenting game, but there are some pretty good guidelines we should pay attention to.

I believe most well-functioning families follow a few fundamental principles, which create the framework to better deal with some of the more insidious problems of parenting. These tools can help us push back on the stress, sorrow, and blame that often come with perfection-driven parenting. If the family is a car, these fundamentals are your socket set. If the family is a garden, these are your spade, hoe, and watering bucket. If you have these tools, you have the ability to address the issues of perfectionism—and the stress, sorrow, and blame that accompany them—that can infect even the seemingly best of families.

But before you whip out this tool set and start cranking or digging or working on whatever needs fixing, there's one critical first step: knowing what—or, in this case, who—you're working with.

Know Your Kids

I'm often surprised by how many parents believe that children are essentially like sugar cookies: give them all the same ingredients, cut them the same way, bake them at the same temperature—and they're bound to come out the same.

Long-time parents know that's not true. Not by a long shot. But even when we know our kids are different, we sometimes get frustrated when they don't have the same talents and aptitudes as their brothers or sisters, or even their parents. If little Lisa is capable of straight A's, well, little Maggie should be able to do the same. If Tommy was homecoming king, Timmy should at least be in the running. This assumption—that our kids all should excel in the same areas (especially if those areas are also important to us parents)—can lead to one of the most damning parental put-downs in our arsenal: "Why can't you be more like [fill in the blank]?"

And even though we know our children differ tremendously from one another, we often still try to use the very same techniques to raise them. We use the same bribes. We unleash the same punishments. We shout at the same volume.

In some ways, this makes sense. It seems fair. We don't want to treat our kids differently, after all. We don't want to show favoritism. But while we may be exceedingly *fair* when we use the same carrots and sticks, we're often not as *effective*. Some children rise to the challenge when Mom pushes them to work harder in school. But some kids might block out the challenge or even come away feeling hopeless.

Some kids might respond to a quiet heart-to-heart but completely rebel when facing a punishment, while other children might need that punishment to get the point. You just don't know—unless you know your kids. Dr. Tim Elmore told me one time that, as a father, he plays chess, not checkers, in his home. "When you play checkers, every piece is alike," he said. "You play chess, you'd better know what each piece can do."

If you followed the checkers assumption, you might assume my two sons, Trent and Troy, would be as alike as they could be. They had the same mom and dad, and they were born just two years apart. They're growing up in the same environment and going to the same school. They needed glasses about the same time, and they do indeed share a lot of the same interests. But spend an afternoon with each of them, and you'll know you're in the company of two very different kids.

Trent, my older son, *looks* more like me. But his personality is more like Jean's, which might help explain why they sometimes clash. He's very thoughtful, very intense. He's super-smart—maybe the smartest one in the whole family, in fact—but he struggles sometimes in school. And even though he looks the most like me in the family, we're very different people.

I played football growing up and played quarterback for my high school in Yucca Valley. I loved the game. Still do. And when Trent was in elementary school, I noticed he was already getting big—looking a lot like I did at that age. And already, I thought, *I bet he's gonna be a football player.* And so when he'd talk about running around with his friends at recess, I'm assuming there are balls involved—footballs, baseballs. There'd have to be, right? He's a Daly kid!

Then one day when he's in fifth grade, Trent comes home from school very, very excited. On top of the world. "Dad!" he says, running up to me. "I won a gold medal!" I'm thinking, *Well, of course you did! You've got your father's athletic genes.*

"All right!" I say. "What did you win it in?"

"Chess!" he says.

I don't think Trent saw that flash of disappointment cross my face, but that's what I felt. *Chess?* I thought. *That doesn't sound like a Daly.* I wasn't disappointed so much by Trent's being involved in chess as by the fact that he wasn't turning into a little mini-me. He might've been my son. He might look like me. But he was turning into his own person. And in that moment, I had a quick decision to make—to encourage him to be more like me or to celebrate his own interests.

"Wow!" I told him. "You got a gold medal in chess? That's INCREDIBLE!"

Troy, meanwhile, looks more like Jean but acts more like me. He's more competitive: Outward accolades, like grades or the praise of his parents, really mean a lot to him. But he's more easygoing too, a lighthearted, joyful, and roll-with-the-punches kind of guy. Trent is less likely to roll with a punch as he is to lean into it—just to prove how much he can take.

Troy seems to excel at almost everything he puts his mind to. And even though Trent has always been the more physically dominant of the two, Troy's actually thicker and in some ways bigger than Trent. Trent is taller but not as hefty. We've got a speed bag and a punching bag down in our basement, and when Troy hits the punching bag, the whole thing moves a few inches. I've been telling Trent lately to not mess with Troy too much. "He's such a nice guy," I say, "but if you push him too far and he lands a punch, he'll knock you out."

You can see their differences really play out in how they've always dealt with physical contact. Troy is Mr. Toucher. All his life, he's loved to hug and to wrestle. He'd plop right in my lap and snuggle into my neck. In fact, even now that he's fourteen, he still does that. He just sits right in my lap as I prep for work in the morning. That kid is a "feel" guy.

But Trent has always been very nonphysical, especially when he was younger. He couldn't hug. If you tried, it was like hugging a cardboard statue. You'd go to hug him, and he wouldn't even put his arms around you.

You can change those inborn characteristics to some extent. When Trent was younger, I told myself, *I'm going to teach this boy how to have tactile interaction. How to touch.* So I went out of my way to caress his back, to tickle him, to run my hands through his hair, to give him a hug every morning when he got up. It was a process. And then before too long, he was the one initiating it. He was coming up and hugging me.

But while you can change your children—bring some of their characteristics into a more healthy equilibrium—you can't change everything about them. They are who they are. The rules and guidelines we impose on them as parents are supposed to help guide them, not change them. Who your children are should dictate how you raise them. How you raise them shouldn't dictate who they are.

It's so important to know who your child is. If you don't know, you're going to miss so much. Those clues are so critical to bonding with that child, to raising that child, to loving that child. They're like a trail of bread crumbs that the Lord puts right in front of you. When you see those bread crumbs, it's important to do something with them. Recognize them. Once you know your children, you can dive into the real work of raising them well. You pull out those tools of yours—the habits you foster, the skills you grow, the little parenting tricks you learn—to coach your boys and girls into becoming the great men and women you know they can be.

Our first tool connects naturally with knowing who your kids are. But it can be one of the toughest to use.

1. Join Their Worlds

Part of knowing who your children are is knowing what they like to do. I think it's important that whenever you can, you try to see their interests and passions through their eyes—to crash their party, join their fun, just as you've always wanted them to join yours.

What parent hasn't wanted to introduce kids into their favorite pastime? If we work on cars, we're bound to give our sons and daughters a socket set for Christmas. If we love to cook, we bring our kids into the kitchen, let them lick the batter off the beaters, and teach them how to crack eggs. If we love fishing, we take our kids fishing. If we love to golf, we take our kids golfing. Many of us Christians are shy about sharing the gospel, but when it comes to passing on our hobbies and passions, we're world-class evangelists.

But just as we like to share our interests with other people, especially our kids, our children want to share with you their own interests—interests they may have developed completely independently of you, by the way. And that can mean we parents have to step outside of our comfort zones, dive into something we're not good at (or don't even *like* particularly), and try to see what our kids enjoy.

It's not easy.

Many of my friends love sports—football, basketball, baseball, everything. Just like I do. They started out as athletes and matured into rabid fans. But somehow, some of my friends' sons didn't get the sports gene. They're not interested at all.

That makes me feel blessed, because my boys share that passion of mine. They like watching and playing football, like their dad. We all love to go hiking. We all love to go camping. We have a lot in common. But we have plenty of differences too.

For instance, Trent really loves art. He's a fantastic sketcher and does what I think are some really good charcoal drawings. His eye for detail is pretty incredible. That's not a skill I have. Frankly, it's not a skill I ever really *wished* I had. While I like a good picture as much as the next guy, I don't have the eye or heart for it like Trent has. I took an art appreciation class in high school, but only because I had to.

But I've really tried to enter into that world of Trent's—to be mindful of his passion and show interest in it. Honestly, I'm still trying to figure out what that looks like—how I can step outside of my world and more into his. It's a process, just like everything. But I'm trying. We've gone to an art museum or two. I've watched him work. And even though I don't share his passion, I'm growing ever more appreciative of his talent.

And like lots of boys their age, Trent and Troy just love video games. Me? Not so much. I can throw a football pretty well, but making a bunch of pixels throw one? Different story. I'm not a great gamer, and if it weren't for my boys, I might not have ever picked up a controller in my adult life. But these days, I'm picking it up quite a bit—throwing a Wii bowling ball down a lane or squealing around an Xbox racetrack with Trent and Troy. Turns out, we have a pretty great time playing those games, even though I wouldn't have chosen to do that on my own. We laugh a lot, even if some of the laughter gets directed at me.

2. Speaking of Laughter . . .

We've already talked about the importance of laughter in my childhood, but I think it's worth a mention here. I think it's so indispensable to find things you and your family can enjoy together, things you can laugh about. Those innocuous little giggles can be pivotal in creating lifelong bonds with your children, fond memories you can share with them forever. Laughter is instrumental in creating a safe space—a critical theme we've already discussed and will return to again and again. This doesn't mean every parent needs to be a comedian. But we all like to laugh, and we all need to have things in our lives that make us laugh.

Sometimes when we're all in the car, the four of us will just start giggling at something we see or say, and we can't stop. We'll laugh and laugh, and pretty soon we'll be laughing at the other people laughing. It has its own momentum, its own delightful spontaneity.

When we laugh, we're at our best. We're in our finest moment. I think the boys would say that too.

But it's important that the laughter is healthy laughter. As much as humor can help heal life's wounds, it sometimes causes them. Humor can be a weapon, cruel and cutting. In many families, humor doesn't bind parents closer to their kids as much as break them apart.

I'm sometimes guilty of this. I can be sarcastic and cutting. Lots of parents can be. We can put down our kids. We can demean them. We make jokes about their appearance or their grades or their work ethic. Sometimes we're trying to make a point; we want to embarrass them, for some reason. Sometimes we just think we're being funny.

And maybe we are. After all, we see that same sort of quick wit on television all the time, don't we? We see the clever asides, the snappy comebacks, the killer put-downs. Entertainment teaches us to engage in a certain kind of mean-spirited humor. And so when we try to use it in our own lives, even with our own kids, it can feel funny. Hey, we might all even laugh. *Did you hear what Dad told Johnny at the dinner table?* But meanwhile, little Johnny's hurting. Little Johnny, in that moment, would rather be anywhere but with Mom and Dad. Suddenly, home isn't such a safe place anymore. And that's the two-edged sword of humor. When used correctly, it can make home feel safe. When it's used to cut or belittle, it feels anything but.

3. Do to Others . . .

My mom never made a big deal out of clean rooms or TV time. She didn't get caught up with a lot of family regulations or household guidelines. There was only one rule she was a stickler for: the Golden Rule: "Do to others what you would have them do to you" (Matthew 7:12).

I don't remember ever being disciplined by my mom for not picking up after myself, bringing home a bad grade, scrawling doodles on the wall, or anything like that. I was a pretty good kid anyway, but if I did get out of line in that way, I don't remember being punished for it. But if I talked back to someone? If I treated someone disrespectfully? That was a whole different story. Practicing good manners and treating people with respect were paramount to her. If we mistreated people, she was all over us.

I think part of it was her Catholic upbringing. She wasn't a religious woman, and we didn't go to church. But she understood what it took to be a good person, and her number one virtue had to do with how to treat people. She saw the Golden Rule as the one rule from which all other rules—the ones worth following, at any rate—came. By teaching kids how to treat people, she figured everything else would fall into place.

The only times I saw my mom angry with me—I mean, *really* angry—was when I was rude to someone else. One time, I'm ashamed to admit, I hit another woman, thinking she was my mother. I thought I'd lost Mom in the grocery store, and when I saw her (or who I *thought* was her), all that fear and anger of being lost welled up inside me, and I hit this stranger hard. When my mom found out about it, she felt horrified. She forced me to apologize in person. It didn't matter that it was an accident, or that I had lashed out because I was scared to death. *You don't mistreat people*, she taught us. *And you never, ever hit them—no matter what.* I still remember the shame I felt in going back to the woman to tell her I was sorry. But my mom did the right thing.

And that's what she always did in those situations. If we broke the Golden Rule, she made sure we took responsibility. It's interesting, because in many ways I was pretty spoiled. I was always the baby of the family, the little boy who could do no wrong. Except, of course, when I did. And when I hurt someone, she made me fess up. I always had to go and ask for forgiveness from the person I hurt. She didn't protect me from that embarrassment. She never apologized for me, never took the blame on herself. She didn't take the responsibility off my shoulders, no matter how old I was. She didn't stand in the gap for me; she didn't make a phone call for me. She made me do it.

A lot of parenting experts might look at my mom and point to all the things she did wrong or could've done better. But in this area— teaching us the Golden Rule and making sure we followed it—Mom was absolutely on point. The Golden Rule, after all, isn't just about treating people with respect and kindness (though, of course, it is that too). It shows us the stark difference between how things *should* work and how, because of our own selfishness, they often don't.

See, we don't always want to follow that rule. Like me in that grocery store, we sometimes want to lash out at people. We want to act selfishly. We want to vent our anger. We want to punish. Something inside us whispers, *If I can make that person feel worse, I'll feel better.* And sometimes, whether we're a child or a parent, we listen to that whisper. We follow it.

The Golden Rule, whether or not we say so, is really an expression of a very important, profound, and difficult Christian ideal: to die to ourselves a little; to live a little for others; to reflect Jesus in some very, very small way in what we say and do.

If you teach the Golden Rule—if you teach your children how to look into their own hearts, to help them see their own weaknesses, their own depravity, their own sinfulness, in a healthy, loving way—I think you've achieved a major thing as a parent. If you and your children can get that down, everything else *does* fall into place. When you're able to make the right decisions in how to interact with and respond to other people, that's a key lesson that'll pay dividends throughout the rest of your life—physically, emotionally, spiritually. *How are you treating people?* my mother asked of us. *How are you treating your friends? How are you addressing that woman? How are you responding to that man? Is that how you'd like to be treated?* And if it wasn't, she was sure to let us know.

4. Be Consistent

My mom's belief in the Golden Rule never wavered. And when we broke it, we knew there would be consequences. I think that's a pretty good lesson too. Even though I don't believe families need a litany of rules to run well, it's important that whatever rules your family does have are consistently enforced.

While my mom was fairly consistent, the men in my life weren't. My birth father was especially erratic because of his drinking. Addictions can tear a family apart in a lot of ways, but it does a particular number on consistency. One night, my dad could be a charming, giving, gentle soul, and the next, he'd threaten my mom and beat my oldest brother. Being with him could be very scary because you never knew exactly what he was going to do. While he never hit me, my brothers and sisters always felt like they had to be hyperaware of everything in his line of sight, watching for the least little thing that might set him off. And any discipline he unleashed was a matter of how he felt right then, in that very moment.

Hank was a little more consistent, but not much. He didn't drink like my dad, but he had a hair-trigger temper. And sometimes his punishments—harsh enough in the best of circumstances—could turn into full-blown rages. One afternoon, I accidentally broke a window in our garage door playing Frisbee, and my sister, Kim, took the blame. Hank took off after her like a demon, shouting curses at her (and she shouting back), and he chased her around and around the yard until she ran down the street. She literally ran away. I didn't see her for about a year.

"The more signals we send of inconsistency, the more it breeds insecurity in a child," Dr. Tim Elmore told me during a broadcast. If we work for a living, we know how important it is to have a consistent boss. Even if he's a bear, you can work with him if you know where you stand and what's important to him. It's just as important when you're a parent, Tim says. After all, your kid can't hand you a letter of resignation if he or she is fed up with you. "I don't think it really matters a lot whether you're overly strict or under—just be consistent," Tim says. "Just be the same, so they know."

Tim acknowledges we can't be perfectly consistent all the time. We have bad days. We make the wrong decision when we're in the heat of things. We'll fall short in this, just as we will everything else. But the more consistent we are, the better off our kids will be—and the more peaceful our home life will feel.

5. Model What You Want to See

Augustin "Augie" Martinez entered the U.S. Marine Corps at eighteen, married the love of his life at twenty-one, and became a father by twenty-three. His son was a bright, intuitive boy who loved his daddy dearly, and before long, the toddler was trying to imitate Augie in every way. Flattering? Yes. Good? Not always.

"He began cursing like I did," Martinez wrote in a letter to Focus on the Family. "One day, at my in-laws' home, Augie [Jr.] let out a few profanities in front of my mother-in-law. My father-in-law is a pastor, and my mother-in-law is a very godly woman. It was at that moment that the realization I had no idea what I was doing as a father lowered itself on me in an ominous dread."

Augie Martinez is hardly the only parent who has been un-intentionally convicted by a sharp-eared kid. I've worked with good moms and dads at Focus on the Family—good *Christian* moms and dads—who, during particularly aggravating trips to preschool, have let out a choice word or two along the way, only to hear those very same words parroted from the car seat behind them. (Or worse yet, received a call from a preschool teacher describing the sort of language that little Suzy has been teaching her classmates.) Your children, especially when very young, turn to you to learn how to interact with the wider world around them. Some research studies have found that by the time infants are even two or three weeks old, they're already beginning to imitate their parents.[1] When you smile, they'll often smile back—like a small, cute mirror. Act like you're upset, and they might cry too. Before they learn to walk or talk, before they can crawl or even hold their head up, they're already learning. They're already watching.

As the child grows, so does their modeling behavior. He might pick up a toy or a banana, hold it up to his ear, and babble into it, because he's seen us do the same with our phones. She might grab a block and point it at the television set, just as she's seen Dad do with a remote control hundreds of times. We might smile when we hear one of our spouse's pet phrases come out of our daughter's mouth—or gasp in horror when, like Augie Martinez, we hear our son curse just like us. Kids idolize their parents, and that idolization lasts for years. They want to be just like Mom and Dad.

If our kids want to be just like us, shouldn't we model behavior that makes us worthy of that devotion? Shouldn't we be the very best role models we can be?

Even when our children don't consciously copy our every word, action, or gesture, we should always remember that they're still watching us. They're still learning from us. And once they hit a certain age, they'll be watching for us to slip up. Adolescents are very attuned to hypocrisy. If they see their parents preach one thing and do something completely different, trust me—they'll notice. Even if they don't call you out on it, they'll notice. And your credibility as a parent will take a hit.

6. Use Your Time Wisely

You may think it's strange for me to talk about time being fundamental to a healthy family, given how little of it I had with my mother. But when you look at all the points I've outlined in this chapter, time is critical to all of them.

You can't know your kids—their strengths and weaknesses, their interests and passions—without spending the time to get to know them. You can't model good behavior for them if you're never around. You pass on the importance of the Golden Rule by showing them how it's practiced, by guiding them in social situations. You teach them how to laugh by laughing with them.

Every lesson we teach takes time. Every memory we make takes time. We need to be with our children on the baseball diamond or in the kitchen, at the study table or in front of the TV. Why do parenting experts constantly affirm the importance of sitting down together for a family meal? Because of the time spent together at that table. Time spent talking, laughing, being with each other.

Time is the currency of the family: How you spend it shows what you value, and who.

Your kids pick up on that sense of value. And while it's great to spend time together as an entire family, it's good to hang out with your individual children too. But it's not always easy, and it's not something the Daly family always does well.

One of the challenges that parents have when their kids are all the same gender or close in age—or, as in my family, both—is that your family time is often a package deal. You all do things together: go to a baseball game together; go to a football game together; go bowling together; go out for pizza together. And even if you love spending time together (like we do), kids relish some alone time with their moms and dads too. When you have, say, a boy or a girl, it's a little more natural to divvy up the time. "Tonight is date night with my daughter," you might say as a father, and your son will understand. He knows you'll probably take him to the ball game next weekend. But when you have two boys close in age, like I do, I'm finding it to be a little harder to split up the time.

But recently, when I told them I wanted to start spending a little more time with each of them individually, I could see their excitement. They showed me they really want that one-on-one time with me. Because if time really is the currency of family, spending time *alone* with your kids makes them feel valued. Important. Loved.

I've started making an effort to do things individually with the boys, and I hope to do more. Maybe golfing with them one-on-one. ATVing. Fishing. It doesn't really matter what we do in some respects, because the time itself is the most important thing. Trent especially seems to open up when we're hanging out together. He has more to share. He's less inhibited. He values that one-on-one time. Some of our best conversations have occurred when it was just me and him, sitting together late at night or going for a drive somewhere.

But there's a catch: while the quantity of the time you spend with your family is important, parents can spend loads of time with their kids and never convey the right stuff. Time spent with children has to be time *well spent*—full of love and laughter, acceptance and forgiveness. If parents spend their "quality" time shaming their children—judging them, demeaning them—it can do more harm than good. If they're spending their time with their kids in a place of utter, dour negativity, that time spent becomes time wasted or worse. Each minute can feel like an hour; a week can feel like a lifetime. The memories made can be bad—bitter ones best forgotten.

Here's the honest truth: It's possible to spend *too much* time with your kids if that's where you're at. Better to leave your children wanting more than wanting less.

Better yet, get out of that space. Make the time precious for all involved. Make the hours you spend with your children fly by rather than stretch out interminably. Time is the greatest currency we have because none of us ever have enough of it. Who we spend it on—and *how* we spend it—says a lot about what we really value.

"I was not a good husband or father," were the opening words of a letter sent to us at Focus on the Family. The author wrote about how he had worked for years as a high-powered executive, "addicted" to work and neglectful of his family. He relocated seven times in eleven years, spending an increasing amount of time away from home, even as he knew his marriage was slowly crumbling.

A friend of his turned him on to Focus on the Family's regular daily broadcasts, and he started listening. He credits our organization with prompting his change of heart. I know God had more to do with it than we did. The man decided that his life needed an overhaul. He needed to spend his precious time on some very precious people.

"I quit my job, moved my family home to Washington, and started a new career with strict boundaries to protect our family life," he wrote. "I dedicated every weekend to my boys. And I started investing in my marriage like never before—planning things for my wife, showing her that I'd been thinking about her. I'm certainly not the perfect husband, but life for our family looks a lot more like it should."

It takes guts to change your life so drastically. I believe it's possible to have both a successful, demanding career and a healthy, happy family. But when your kids are taking a backseat to your career or other outside demands, there's a toll involved. And the courageous moms and dads who overturn their careers for the sake of their families rarely regret it.

Time is so critical to a healthy, well-running family. It feeds into so many fundamentals that it can be seen as the most critical fundamental of all. Whether we have a lot of it to spend or just a few precious minutes a day, we've got to spend it wisely.

And there's no better use of time in my opinion than to use it in conversation.

7. Talk . . .

I sometimes wonder how many parents talk with their children. Sure, we talk *at* them a lot. We tell them what to do and how to act. We suggest, we cajole, we demand. Like pastors at the pulpit, we preach. But how often do we *listen* to our children? We want to give our children so much—our experience, our perspective, our understanding of how things should be done. But sometimes we forget that our kids want to give us their perspective too. They need to. They're more than sponges ready to absorb whatever we want to spill their way; they're people, like their parents, who are dealing with lots of their own stuff. And if we really want to help them, we must do more than talk. We must listen. Really listen.

A mom and her soon-to-be teenage son—we'll call them Maddie and Justin—were picking up some supplies for Justin's thirteenth birthday sleepover party. After filling their cart with all the junk food it could carry ("you have your thirteenth birthday slumber party only once, right?" Maddie says), they climbed back into the car and flipped on the radio. A Focus on the Family broadcast was playing. "I heard the speaker say something about parents wanting our junior high kids to listen to us," Maddie says, "but they want us to listen to them too."

. Maddie reached over and flipped off the station, thinking the last thing Justin wanted to listen to was Christian talk radio. But to her surprise, Justin turned it back on. They listened to the show the rest of the way home. And then as the two pulled into their driveway, Justin suddenly turned to his mother.

"Mom, that's how I feel sometimes," he said. "I feel like . . . I just want you to really listen to me. Like, when we're in an argument. That's how I feel. I just want you to take me seriously."

Maddie calls the conversation that followed "brief but wonderful." Both mom and son came to a new understanding. Maddie promised she'd try to listen to him and speak to him in a way that showed she really was listening. She'd hear his side of the story. She'd treat Justin like a regular person—even if that regular person might still be grounded after the conversation.

"My son and I have a very good relationship, I think," she later wrote to Focus, "but this teenager stuff *is* difficult. For both of us."

Maddie's right—this "teenager stuff" is hard. Sometimes it can feel almost impossible. But when I'm at my best with my two teenage boys, it's when we're talking. Listening. Engaging with each other.

This is another area where a few important fundamentals come into play: You have to take the *time* to engage. You have to *know* your kids. Children, especially teenagers, don't always feel like talking. So when they do, you have to be ready to take advantage of those times.

Trent tends to get chatty later in the evening. When the clock hits ten or eleven, and I'm having trouble keeping my eyes open, Trent might suddenly turn conversational. He'll start talking about school and his friends. He'll talk about his feelings and dreams and wishes. And even as tired as I might be, I think, *Man, this is great! A real conversation with my son!* Just a few nights ago, Trent and I spent forty-five minutes talking freely and openly. We talked about grades, which he's been struggling with, but I wasn't angry and he wasn't defensive. I tried very hard to make the conversation constructive, *not instructive,* and a big part of creating the right atmosphere for a real talk with our kids is to be willing to listen. Hey, at this point, we both knew the score. He and I both understand that doing homework and keeping up in school are important to Jean and me. It's not as if I

yell about it one more time Trent will suddenly say to himself, *Wow.
Guess Dad really cares about this stuff. Guess I'll work harder from here
on.* No perfect decibel level will suddenly make all of your great advice
seep into their brains and be perfectly applied. No, the longer I'm a
parent, the more I'm convinced that it tends to work the opposite way.
Sometimes you're at your most convincing—you're at the height of
your power as a parent—when you don't talk at all. You listen. And
when you *do* talk, you talk to your kids like they're among the most
important people in your life.

And that should be easy to do, because they are.

I have a heart for evangelism. I think at my core that's who I
am—an evangelist. I love engaging people who don't know the Lord,
even when they're overtly hostile to the idea of God. This may sound
strange, but I feel a real sense of God's peace in those moments. I don't
get emotional; I don't get defensive; I don't get red in the face. Even
when people attack me in that environment, it doesn't especially bother
me. In those spaces, I try my best to reflect what I imagine Jesus to be
like: kind, patient, loving, firm, gracious. I try to listen. And when I
talk, I try to keep in mind *how* I'm speaking and who I'm speaking
to. Not always perfectly, I need to add.

You wouldn't necessarily think that parenting and evangelism
would have that much in common. But I wonder now, as I write this,
whether the two have some similarities.

In a way, maybe we're evangelizing our kids—not into the kingdom of God (though, of course, we do that too), but into the world of
responsible adulthood. We want to love them. We want to save them.
We want to prepare them for the challenges ahead and show them the
beauty of what lies in front of them.

So from that perspective, what does parenting look like? It's
patient. It's kind. It's generous in spirit. It's all those things.

So when I enter into a conversation with my kids—and when I'm
at my best—I think I act a little like an evangelist. I'm low-key. I ask
questions and listen to the answers. In a way, I try to win their hearts.

But let me stress, those great conversations can't be had for the asking. They can't be forced. One night, Trent will talk my ear off, and the next, it'll sound more like . . .

"How's it going?"

"Good."

"What'd you do today?"

"Nothing."

One night, the conversation really flows, and the next, it's all pins and needles. In Trent's case, it has a lot to do with stress. When it loads up on him, he quiets down, and you can't do anything to pry the words out. You can't expect to have great conversations all the time, any more than you can expect to be a perfect parent. So don't force it.

Unless of course you have to. Because sometimes you *do* have to force conversations. You have to confront a problem or tackle a subject that just can't wait. Even when the words don't come easy—when both you and your child would rather be anywhere else—those can be the most important words to share.

7a. . . . Even When It's Hard

One of Trent's schoolmates killed himself this year. He played on the football team. Trent practiced with him every day. We got a note from the school, asking us to talk with our child about it. We needed to make sure our kids were OK, the letter said. And if they weren't, the school offered free counseling.

But it's hard to talk to your child about suicide. For many parents, bringing up the topic feels awkward, even intrusive. I have a pretty good relationship with my boys, but it wasn't easy for me either. I asked Trent how he was doing. *How well did you know the boy? How are you dealing with his death?* I circled nearer the most serious, most difficult question of all. *Did his death make you think about suicide too?*

"I'm good," he said. "I don't really feel affected by it. I don't

know why he did it, and it's sad he did it, but I'd never do something like that."

He said all the right things, all the things that make a dad breathe a sigh of relief.

That same conversation got repeated in lots of houses around the school district that evening. Many parents likely heard the same sorts of answers. "I'm good. It's sad. I'd never do something like that."

That's what we want and expect to hear. And because of that, there's a temptation to not even start the conversation, to close it down before a word even gets spoken. Some parents might tell themselves, *My son's just fine. He's acting just the same, talking just the same. There's no need to talk about it. No need to make us both feel uncomfortable.*

But some parents received much different and more difficult answers.

A friend of mine talked with his own boy, a classmate of Trent's and a member of the football team, about the suicide that night. His conversation probably started out a lot like mine did: "Did you know him well? Are you doing all right?" Maybe he thought he knew what his son would say before he said it. Maybe he figured his boy would say, like Trent did, "I'm good."

But his boy didn't say that. Instead, he said this: "Dad, you need to stop traveling. You're not home enough for me."

You're not home enough for me. You need to be home. I need you. Words spoken in the context of a classmate's suicide.

To this father's credit, he quit his job and got another one that didn't require so much travel. Just like that. He's spending more time on the people he values most.

But his experience touches me deeply. How many parents might never have had that difficult conversation with their sons and daughters because they assumed their kids were just fine? How many children long for the chance to tell their parents something hard, something important? *I'm not good. I'm hurting. I need you. Help me.*

And how many children told their parents just what they wanted to

hear? How many kids might've said all the right things . . . but didn't mean them? We parents protect our kids from uncomfortable truths all the time. Sometimes our children do the same with us.

After hearing my friend's story, I started thinking about Trent's response, how much he sounded like I might have at his age. "I'm good," I would've said, even when I wasn't. So as uncomfortable as it felt, I doubled back to that conversation.

"Trent, are you sure you're OK?" I asked him.

I could see he felt irritated. "Yeah, Dad, I'm fine," he said. "I'm not in that place, and I won't be."

I believe him. But at the same time, I'm not completely sure. Teens don't always tell their parents everything. Do I know everything I should? Am I doing everything I can?

That's the thing about these so-called fundamentals: They, like everything else in parenting, can be frustratingly squishy. Even when we're aware of them—when we're doing them to the best of our ability—a nagging question always tags along, perhaps unspoken but never far from our mind. I know my kids . . . *but do I know them well enough?* I spend time with my kids . . . *but is it the right kind of time?* I talk with my kids . . . *but how can I be sure I'm listening to what's really important? Am I asking the right questions? Picking up the right cues? Is there something I'm missing?*

As I said at the beginning, there is no set rule book to parenting, no list to follow, no guidelines to guarantee (or your money back) parenting success. To be a parent is to have a thousand questions tugging on what can seem like every last brain cell, causing you to wonder and doubt. No one parent can answer all these questions or lay aside all these fears.

Maybe that's why God designed us to have two parents in play.

Chapter Five

OPPOSITES ATTRACT

✦

Before we had children to love, most of us fell in love with someone else. We likely cemented that love and commitment to each other in front of a pastor or judge. We promised to love and cherish our partner in good times and bad, in sickness and in health, until death do us part.

Maybe we should think about adding to those traditional vows. Maybe we should promise to have and to hold our spouses through the terrible twos and the teenage years, through soccer practices and parent-teacher conferences and prom nights. In some families, children can be the glue that helps hold families together. But in others, they can be the crowbar that torques them apart.

Let me be very transparent with you. That's sometimes the case in my family. Jean and I love each other a great deal. We love our two kids with all of our being. But when Jean and I have strong disagreements, it's often over how to deal with the boys.

Let me give you a little peek into what the Daly household might look like on a weeknight at, say, 6:00 p.m.:

I pull into the driveway, and Jean, a work-at-home mom, is busy around the house. As soon as I step in the door, she begins to give me the day's status report and the evening's marching orders.

"Trent's still struggling in algebra," she might say. "He needs to study more, and he's not listening to me. You need to talk with him.

And you must tell the boys that they've *got* to get their rooms cleaned up tonight.

"Oh," she adds with a hug, "welcome home."

These little "welcome home" meetings stress me out. Because— and I know I might get in trouble for being so honest—I don't *care* that much about their rooms. My mom never bothered much about whether or not I made my bed. I've never been at a job interview where Human Resources marked me down for "insufficient household tidiness." And while I care about algebra as much as the next guy, I'm not sure that lecturing Trent is going to help much. In fact, another lecture might make it worse. I figure the best thing I can do is come in, be as lighthearted as possible, and maybe say something funny and make everyone feel at ease.

But for Jean, *the other stuff matters*. She grew up in a family that encouraged and expected the kids to excel, and the girls particularly did so marvelously. She believes that families should be built around mutual respect, and part of that respect comes from following the family rules—to clean rooms, to work hard, to honor Mom and Dad by being the best kids possible. And when she perceives the kids are not doing their best, she'll let them know it, sometimes by asking *me* to tell them.

The way I look at it, Jean's a little more of an Old Testament parent than I am. For her, rules are rules, and we should never break them. I'm more a New Testament kind of guy. I not only tend to think in terms of grace; I absolutely rely on it.

That's how I see things, but not Jean. She has a totally different perspective. Forget that Old Testament/New Testament stuff. "Jim is just way too soft," she'd say. "It makes my job harder. He forces me to be the bad cop all the time. And that gets really tiring for me." She believes she needs to compensate for my weakness, my desire to be liked and be the good guy. And you know what? There's a lot of truth in that scenario too.

If we were looking to buy an M-rated video game for the boys like

Call of Duty, for example, Jean might call it too violent and therefore inappropriate for kids our boys' ages. Meanwhile, I'd say, "Hey, it looks fun. Let's get it!" I get frustrated because Jean won't let us have our game. She gets frustrated because I'm just too laid-back, too permissive. And then when she asks me to "step up my game," my frustration level rises even more because she's pushing me into a place where I don't feel all that comfortable. And maybe I don't even agree with it.

Sometimes we can laugh about these differences, but sometimes it can create real friction in our family. While Jean and I agree in many areas and do our best to present a united front to the boys, it sometimes can feel like we're operating from manuals featuring totally conflicting instructions and written in completely different languages. We're *very* different parents, Jean and I. We're very different *people*.

Sometimes it's easy to forget that those very differences make us so good together. I believe the Lord wanted us together in the first place because of those differences.

It Takes Two

Jean couldn't have had a more different childhood than I did. She came from a very tight-knit, well-educated family—not Christians, but they shared many Christian values, especially family togetherness. They hunted together. They camped together. They skied together. Two of Jean's siblings became world-class skiers. In a way, that drive to succeed reflects another family trait: they excelled together. I sense that excellence was pretty much expected of them. About the time she came into my life in the early 1980s, she had become a Christian and had already hopped on the fast track to fulfilling her goals—a biology major, a veterinary assistant, and an animal lover going to Cal State Fullerton with an eye toward becoming a veterinarian. Jean doesn't waste time.

We were both California kids, born and raised. But we might as well have grown up on opposite points on the globe. We might well have never met, except for some well-meaning interference from friends.

A friend of mine, Dan, was dating a girl named Tina, who knew Jean in high school. They thought we'd hit it off. She was a left-brained, intellectual achiever, while I was the right-brained, footloose spontaneous type. Maybe they hoped that if we got together, we might have a full brain between us.

Not like *that* was ever going to happen.

Neither of us were dating at the time. In high school, despite my Christian faith, I didn't have many boundaries. While I was no wild thing, when it came to girls I strayed outside the boundaries. But after I returned from studying for a year in Japan in 1983, I decided I needed to stop all that. I saw it as spiritually unhealthy for me.

And Jean? Well, Jean was beautiful. Every guy wanted to be with her, and she had grown tired of dealing with all the pressure that came with dating. She had decided to wait for the mate God had chosen for her. Despite the best efforts of Dan and Tina, therefore, it looked as though Jean and I would go our separate ways without ever setting eyes on each other.

Things went better for Dan and Tina. They got engaged and scheduled their wedding for June 1985. The Wednesday night before the wedding, I went to a church service at Lake Arrowhead Christian Fellowship, a church I'd visited maybe only three or four times before. During the worship service, the pastor came up to me and said, "I have a word from the Lord for you."

I wasn't used to that kind of thing. *Sure you did*, I thought. But I asked him for the word—just to be polite.

The pastor told me what he sensed the Lord saying to me: "I've got your mate picked out for you, and she's going to have a heart for the things of God."

Well.

People tell me I must've been on the lookout for my future spouse, but that's simply not true. Do you know my first thought when the pastor told me God wanted to play matchmaker for me? *What insanity is this?* followed by, *I'm not going back to that church again.* And remember, I was in a no-dating mode.

Dan and Tina's wedding rolled around three days later. I went without a date and spent much of the reception hanging out with my friends. But as the guests snacked on cake and danced to the band, Dan walked up to me. "I've got someone I'd like to introduce you to," he said. He led me over to Jean. I asked if she would like to dance, and she said yes.

We danced one time. That was it. She later told me she felt uncomfortable because she had come to the wedding with a guy friend and didn't want to ignore him. We danced once, and then she walked away.

I strolled back to my table and sat next to my friend, Victor. "I think that's the woman I'm going to marry," I told him.

Compatible?

That one dance certainly caught my interest. Jean didn't have close to the same sense of conviction. And when Dan and Tina, ever our romantic helpmates, encouraged us to see each other again, Jean tried to beg off.

Maybe it's for the best, I thought. I'd sworn off dating anyway. But for some reason, Jean finally relented. We went on an "unofficial" double date with Dan and Tina. I packed a picnic dinner, and then we went to see an Amy Grant concert at the Pacific Amphitheatre. Despite the great entertainment, the only thing that mattered to me, the only thing I even noticed, was Jean, standing beside me. She looked so beautiful, seemed so charming, so . . . everything.

That night, for the first time, Jean started to get the sense that I might be the one too. From then on, we clicked. No more no-dating mode for either of us.

Of course, those early dates looked a bit different than you might expect.

She was so beautiful—she still is—and I think most of the guys she dated were very interested in getting to know her in *that* way. As a Christian, Jean wanted none of that and had grown tired of that sort of pressure. Given my past, I knew all about the sort of sexual pressure that so often goes along with a romantic relationship. I wanted something different, for both her and me. I wanted to honor God in this relationship. So for the first couple of dates, I just shook her hand at the door. Then, after a while, we'd end our evenings with a kiss on the cheek. I didn't kiss her on the lips for *months*, but by that time, I knew I wanted to marry her. So when she switched colleges and transferred to the University of California, Davis, located way up north near Sacramento, I quit my job to follow her. Because my brother and his wife lived in Sacramento, I rented a room from them to stay close to my girl.

We spent most of that school year cementing our relationship. Fantastic! We thought we were totally in sync with one another. We enjoyed the same activities and laughed at the same jokes. Dan and Tina may have thought we operated out of two different brains, but Jean and I felt as though we were of the very same soul.

One day that spring, while Jean and I hung out at my brother's house, I got a call from Paul Fullwood, a friend from Australia who'd recently taken a job with a Christian group called Motivational Media. The group ran a program encouraging high school kids to stay away from drugs and alcohol. Twenty teams, each made up of two people, traveled the country in custom vans, visited local high schools, set up a multimedia show, and told kids about the dangers of drug and alcohol abuse. Paul asked if I knew anyone who'd be interested in joining the team.

Hmmm. Groups of two.

"You're together all the time, right?" I asked.

"Yeah," he said.

"Do you do couples?"

"Only if they're married."

"Of course," I said. "Hang on." I put the phone to my chest and turned to Jean.

"Do you want to get married and spend the next year traveling around the country telling kids about drug and alcohol abuse?"

Remember, Jean is the practical one. The planner. The person who had a four-year dating and engagement plan for marriage. She studied things like biochemistry for her degree, for cryin' out loud. Even then, I knew that spontaneity wasn't exactly a part of her makeup.

"Well," she said, "could we give him the answer tomorrow?"

We called Paul back the next day and said we'd take the job. The training began three weeks later. We had that much time to allow Jean to finish finals, plan a wedding in six weeks, and then have both of us move back temporarily from Northern Cal to Southern Cal.

Everything went surprisingly smoothly. Jean finished her finals. We booked our ideal wedding location, thanks to a last-minute cancellation. Everything just fell into place, just like we assumed our wedded life would. Oh, we knew marriage would have its share of challenges. But we also knew they'd be mere bumps on the road to happiness. After all, it felt like Jean and I were so alike!

We were in for quite a surprise.

Discovering Differences

Several months before Jean and I got married, even before we set a date, we figured we would get married. We even enrolled in a premarital counseling session, which met for eight hours every Saturday for three weeks. Naturally, you learn a lot about each other during those heavy, soul-baring discussions.

For some couples, it was too much.

A good chunk of the course focused on unearthing differences, potential friction points, between the would-be husband and would-be wife. Of the ten couples who walked in with us, three opted not to get married after all. They decided they were just too different, I guess, to wake up next to each other every day for the rest of their lives.

Jean and I, on the other hand, walked out of the sessions feeling pretty good. After all, we seemed so similar in so many ways. As Christians, we shared a great deal already, including priorities centered around our faith. We had the same ultimate hope. Moreover, we had similar journeys to that faith. And, of course, we shared so many of the same interests: athletics and being outdoors, keeping up with the news and current events, a similar sense of humor. We even liked the same food.

But in the months and years after we got married, we began to see a lot of differences too. I was the spontaneous extrovert, married to a meticulous, planning introvert. We came to realize that, even if we both enjoyed hiking, camping, tennis, and keeping up on the news of the day, we sometimes didn't feel much alike at all. In those times, especially stressful times, it didn't seem as though I came from Mars and she came from Venus. It felt like we came from the opposite ends of the galaxy.

Still, the fact that we differed so greatly didn't make us unfit to marry each other. It didn't make us unsuitable to stay together. It just meant we had some extra challenges in front of us. Although we may struggle at times with the things that make us different, those very things can make us even stronger. They can make us *better* together.

It's part of the balance of things. There's a reason that opposites attract—spiritually, emotionally, even scientifically. We sometimes fill different roles. We sometimes meet different needs. You can even see it in the dynamics of the family. One parent leans toward nurturing, another to teaching. One may excel at creating a safe place in the family; another may encourage her kids to push the boundaries. And both are important! I believe it demonstrates God's design for the family and for our relationships. You naturally seek what you don't possess. A free-spirited person may subconsciously seek stability in a mate to help provide much-needed security. An introvert may fall in love with an extrovert, somehow knowing that she can help him break out of his shell. You end up finding each other.

Sure, you may share a lot of similarities. You may love the same foods or feel crazy about the same vacations. But at your core, you're wired differently. And you need the help of someone else to make you complete. As Jesus says in Mark 10:8, "So they are no longer two, but one flesh." We don't just *love* each other. Spiritually, somehow, I think we can make each other better.

It's not wholly unlike what we find in the business world. When you take a personality test as part of a work group—the DiSC assessment or the Myers-Briggs Type Indicator or any of a number of others—almost certainly you'll hear that a great team is made of many different personality types. Each person brings their own strengths and weaknesses to the table. Our strengths bring strength to the team. Our weaknesses offset other people's strengths. Sure, working with very different people can challenge us. We may wish that everyone saw the world the same way we do. And it's true, many studies suggest that teammates should share some traits and inclinations. We need those to communicate and function.

But differences, not similarities, power a team to the next level. Our differences force us to think about problems in different ways and find creative, out-of-the-box solutions. Yes, our differences challenge us. But when we yoke our differences and work toward a shared goal, marvelous things can result. We just need to be willing to put in a little more time and effort and go into that environment accepting and valuing those differences. If we try to force someone into seeing the world in our way, it won't work. We are who we are. God made us that way and we must assume that He likes it that way. He must *like* our differences. He must *like* us to balance each other out—in our friendships, our workplaces, and, most especially, in our marriages.

Jean and I walked into marriage thinking, *Wow, we're so much alike!* But after a couple of years, we realized, *Wow, we have some differences. But you know what? Our love makes up for all that. We can make it work.* And we have.

But it hasn't always been easy.

Rocky Roads

I loved the year Jean and I spent on the road doing our antidrug talks. I loved every minute we spent together, and we were together *all the time*. For the first time in my life, I had someone I could count on to be there when I woke up, to be there when I went to sleep. For maybe the first time since I was five years old, I knew what family should feel like.

Little did I know I was driving Jean crazy. I might've loved being with her 24/7, but Jean needed her space.

About four months in, Jean announced that she had to run to the grocery store.

"Great!" I said. "I'll come with you."

"No, no, no," Jean finally said, a hint of exasperation in her voice. "Can I just go by myself?"

I said yes, of course. But even though I said I understood that Jean needed some "me" time, I still felt a little hurt. It felt like Jean preferred the company of ground beef and frozen broccoli to me. I didn't yet understand one of the real differences between extroverts like me and introverts like Jean. I recharge when I'm with people, and there's nobody I'd rather be with than Jean. Introverts need time alone to recharge. Time with people, even people they love, can drain them. Jean had been constantly "on" for four months straight. She needed some time to recharge, even if she had to do it while shopping for cereal.

It wasn't the only time we experienced dissonance in our relationship. About fifteen years ago, shortly after we had Trent, we decided to give a rating to our marriage. Was it healthy? Was it satisfying?

I had no doubt it was. Sure, it wasn't perfect, but I gave it a nine—a solid A—and I thought I was being maybe overly critical.

Jean looked at my rating. "A nine?" she said. "You're kidding. We're at, like, a two."

That's when I learned about another core difference between Jean and me. You wouldn't necessarily know it from the books I write, but

Jean can feel that I'm too emotionally reserved. Even though I can talk about some difficult moments in my life, both past and present, I rarely let it touch me emotionally. She believes I find it hard to be truly vulnerable. It's hard for me to allow her full access into the emotional side of who I am.

My resiliency? My ability to cope with problems? Jean would say those positive traits come with another, more negative edge. As a child, I learned how to wall off that part of me from the rest of my waking, conscious world. And perhaps she's right. I don't know if it's healthy, but I just don't go there.

I've tried to improve. I don't think Jean would rate our marriage a two anymore. We're as much in love as ever. But it's still not perfect. Even though I've worked at making myself more vulnerable, she'd still argue I have a ways to go. She wants a key to that room, that room where she believes I keep my pain locked up. She wants to go there. She wants to help. But from my perspective, I don't think I even know what's *in* that room. I don't even know if the room *exists*. I never open that door.

Fifteen years later, we still deal with this issue. Maybe we'll be working on it for the next fifteen years. And the next fifteen. Until death do us part?

Most marriages have long-standing issues, problems that haunt them again and again. It's part of living and loving people who differ from you, people who sometimes see the world from very different angles. And while those issues may never fully disappear, husbands and wives must always work on them. If we want to create a healthy family, we need to start with a healthy marriage.

Come On, Baby, Light My Fire

I've talked several times on the Focus on the Family broadcast with marriage expert Ted Cunningham, the founding pastor of Woodland

Hills Family Church in Branson, Missouri. He believes the bond between husband and wife spiritually supersedes the bond between parent and child, bonds we often reverse today. As parents, we unwittingly place our children at the head of the table. We make them the center of our lives, even though our primary job as parents is to get them to a place where they leave our homes and live happy, healthy lives on their own. He stresses that putting marriage first doesn't mean loving your kids any less. When we prioritize our relationship with our spouse, it puts us in a position to love our kids more.

On a recent broadcast, he talked about the traditional unity candle that plays a role in most marriage ceremonies. "It's one of the greatest object lessons at a wedding, because you have the two individual candles representing the bride and groom—husband and wife," he says. "And those are your personal spiritual journeys before the Lord. The center of the candle equals the unity candle. It's where you come together.

"And then I always love to pull out of my jacket or out of a drawer near the candle, a bunch of little white birthday candles, representing the children," he adds. "You're one day going to have a bunch of little candles running around the house. And they're going to be tapping into all of these flames—Mom's spiritual journey, Dad's spiritual journey, and the marriage journey. It's important that we model this every single day before our kids. And so, don't neglect that marriage journey."

Cunningham laments the fact that so many couples get divorced today. They swear they'll try to protect their children from the breakup. But when the fire of a marriage gets snuffed out, it's bound to impact the kids. Inevitably they feel it.

"I hear it too much as a pastor," he said. "'We're divorcing, but we'll stay friends for the kids.' I always say the same thing. 'If you can stay friends, you can stay married.'"

I agree.

Now, I'm not saying that single parents can't be great parents. Although it's harder statistically, it can be done. They can raise healthy, well-functioning kids. Nevertheless, it all comes back to the title of this chapter: "Opposites Attract." We need those opposites to create a fully formed, functioning family environment. We need those two halves to make a whole family. When one of those halves leaves the picture or shows up just for the weekends, the kids can't help but feel those repercussions.

It reminds me of another unity candle story.

One of my friends reports that when he and his wife tied the knot, their "unity candle" was actually two halves of one larger candle. "We didn't light the center candle and blow out our candles," he says. "We instead put the two halves together—each of us still having our own separate wick, but now burning together and creating a bigger flame."

I see a lot of truth in that sort of ceremony. Yes, when we marry, we become one. But we're also two very different people. And no matter how long the marriage lasts, that marriage will always be made of two different folks. Marriage unites a man and a woman, but it doesn't squash us into one being. We are one *and* two. Indivisible individuals, hopefully.

But we know it doesn't always work out like that. When we picture marriage as my friend's divided unity candle, I think we can better see what divorce can really look like. We can remove one half of the candle and the other half will still burn. It can still give light to all of Ted Cunningham's tiny birthday candles. But it won't burn as well or as brightly. It'll look off. Lopsided. Like something's missing.

From my perspective, the goal is to stay together always. To take that vow we make before the Lord—"to have and to hold . . . until death do us part"—as a concrete, unbreakable promise. Barring physical abuse or infidelity, most of the problems we face in marriage can be overcome. And even in the case of those two latter, horrific issues, I believe there still can be hope.

Don't stay together only for the kids' sake! Stay together for your *own* sake.

A while back, the University of Chicago studied couples, both married and divorced, to explore whether divorce actually led to greater happiness. The scientists had an emphatic answer: No.[1] They found that unhappy married couples who got divorced were on average, five years later, still unhappy—just as miserable, in fact, as the unhappy couples who stayed married. Divorced men and women didn't get a perceptible bump in their self-esteem. If they felt depressed before the divorce, they still felt depressed afterward.

As men and women, we tend to look for happiness outside ourselves. "Oh, this person will make me happy," we say. "This thing will satisfy me." And in some respects, when it comes to marriage, there's some truth in that. I can say definitively that I'm happier with Jean than without her.

But at the same time, that way of thinking can lead to a trap. Our unhappiness must be someone else's fault. And that can lead some people into looking for happiness outside their marriage.

If I just got that other girl, she'd understand, men think. *My life would be easier.* And then they marry that other girl and discover they still have the same stinking problem.

It's like the old cliché that humorist Erma Bombeck used to take exception to: "The grass is always greener on the other side." It's not, really, she'd insist. In fact, "The grass is always greener over the septic tank"[2]—it's always greener where you water it. Water the grass where you are.

Back to the Basics

But *how* do you water it? How can you foster a quality marriage that sets the cadence for the rest of the family? How can you create an environment where your love doesn't just survive but has a chance to glow and spread? How can you fix a broken marriage?

I went into greater detail on how to foster a healthy marriage in my book *Marriage Done Right.*[3] But for our purposes, I'd like to concentrate on a few big keys—elements that echo, not surprisingly, the fundamentals I outlined just one chapter ago.

Know your spouse. This may sound counterintuitive, since we clearly already know them so well. But do we? Do we truly know what brings them joy? What wounds they've suffered? Their happiest childhood memory? Their greatest fear? And sometimes, even when we *do* know them well, over the years we sometimes forget. We lose sight of who they are and what they love, even what they love about us. Sometimes because they've become such an overwhelming, constant presence in our lives, we almost forget what they look like. They begin to blend in with everything else we see every day. And while a certain beauty comes with that level of intimate familiarity, a danger lurks there too. We can never lose sight of the reasons we wanted to spend the rest of our lives with the person across the table from us. Sometimes we have to reacquaint ourselves with that person, to get to know them all over again.

Join their worlds. I know not every guy loves to go fabric shopping with his quilt-mad wife. Not every woman will understand why her husband needs to watch three football games every Sunday. Not every spouse will understand their partner's irrational love of hunting and fishing or their desire to attend Zumba classes or their strange impulse to dress up like Boba Fett for Star Wars movie premieres. But even if we can't share a particular passion, I think it's important at least to try to understand that passion and enter into it whenever possible. Your spouse loves you. He loves certain things. When you show your spouse that you'd like to understand (and even, when possible, share that love), it can reset a relationship in the best of ways. It can remove a point of possible friction and turn it into a joint activity. Even if you can't fully embrace an activity—I know men who'd rather go on a twenty-mile forced march than participate in a Zumba class—at least you can appreciate that it nourishes something important inside your spouse.

But let me add a couple of caveats. First, don't encourage healthy passions to become unhealthy obsessions. As much as I love football, spending ten hours on a Sunday watching it probably doesn't do much for my marriage or my family. Moderation is the key. Second, be careful not to force your way into these worlds. I always recall Jean's need to go to the grocery store without me. Sometimes these separate worlds provide healthy opportunities for your husband or wife to have a little time for themselves.

Laugh. Never forget that God intends us to love these lives He's given us and to enjoy our lives in union. The pressures of career, family, and relationships can feel overwhelming, and part of being in a marriage means sharing those difficult burdens. But just as important is the opportunity to share the good times. It's important to make memories together. I find that some of my happiest, most treasured memories with Jean are filled with laughter. And naturally, when we recall those memories, the recollections echo with laughter too. As couples, we need to remember to giggle. Watch a favorite comedy. Rib each other over a funny, shared embarrassment. Share a private joke. To laugh with your significant other can, even at seemingly its most shallow, provide a salve to cool a bit of heartache. And if you share enough laughter, it can become an integral part of the cement that holds together your relationship.

Follow the Golden Rule. Common sense would tell us to treat our husbands and wives with the same respect and courtesy we'd expect from them. But sometimes we forget. The old cliché speaks some truth: we always hurt the ones we love. The cliché seems unthinkable in the early days of marriage. *Hurt the love of my life? Never!*—but wedded vets will tell you it happens all too easily. In our very worst moments, it can even feel *tempting.* Our differences can make husband and wife a better team, but they can also drive us a little crazy. Sometimes we don't want to win arguments so much as we want to shame the other person. We want them to submit to our superior intellect so they'll never disagree with us again. We may try to "win" by bringing up old, hurtful memories, by picking at particularly painful scabs, or by probing for insecurities. Sometimes we fight through sheer volume. And in some marriages, sadly, disagreements can become exponentially worse.

It's hard to remember the warmth of your unity candle in the heat of battle, but try! It's important.

Look for opportunities to express your love, friendship, and gratitude in unsought, unexpected ways. Offer a back rub. Take on a cleaning chore you don't typically do. Fix a special meal. We may say we'd sacrifice everything for our spouses, and yet so often we grumble when our spouse asks us to pick up milk or call a plumber. Likewise, if your spouse does something special for you, *take notice*. These gestures are important and meaningful. Don't take their kindness for granted.

Talk. To know each other takes conversation. To laugh together involves talk. Almost every marriage expert will tell you that communication is the key to every healthy marriage, and it becomes even more crucial when problems pop up, which they inevitably do. Sometimes you need to deal with little things, like your husband leaving his shoes in the middle of the floor. Sometimes the conversations grow big, as when you need to confront a spouse over an addiction to alcohol, drugs, or porn. And sometimes it's about ongoing conflicts, like the conflicts Jean and I have over our boys.

Whether the issues are big or small, though, it's important not to ignore the issues. We mustn't withdraw, as many men tend to do in these situations. At times, spouses do more than withdraw; they roll over. They cave in on these issues instead of engaging with them in a healthy way. Since they don't want the fight or the drama, they just say, "OK, have it your way," and go back to the television set.

Some marriages run into trouble right there. One partner just ends up rolling over all the time. It might last for a decade or two, maybe three, until finally they say, "I don't think I love you anymore." They've rolled over so much that they're incapable of feeling *anything* for the person they swore to love and cherish for the rest of their lives.

Finding Delight in the Differences

None of these fundamental tools will solve what can sometimes feel like the prickliest problem of all: the underlying differences between husband and wife. To get past that issue, couples need more than laughter or a commitment to take up running together. They need patience and grace and, most importantly, an understanding that their spouse's differences are assets, not liabilities. The fact that we're wired differently from each other is part of God's design for our lives, not a cosmic mistake.

Even the experts can find this truth hard to come to terms with. When Dr. Jill Savage, a speaker and author of the book *Hearts at Home*, appeared on the Focus on the Family broadcast in 2013, she candidly described the struggles she and her husband, Mark, had during their twenty-five years of marriage (and counting).

"There were a lot of dynamics that were causing that to happen," she said. "One was that, honestly, Mark and I were working really hard to change each other instead of accepting each other as who we really were as individuals. And so when we saw each other doing something different from the way we would do it, instead of seeing it as *different*, we were seeing it as *wrong*."

They also had different ways of dealing with conflict. "I would withdraw," Savage admitted, "and he would rage."

It sounds a lot like how LeRoy and Kimberly Wagner described their own marital journey on a broadcast two years later. LeRoy, a pastor, always fought to make Kimberly more organized, just like he was. Kimberly, author of the book *Fierce Women*, would see LeRoy's own differences as weaknesses. "And that," she said, "would tend to cause me to have a superior attitude toward him."

Like Jill Savage and her husband, those differences got further exacerbated by a disconnect in communication. "The more she would come at me with her opinions or what she was wanting to get across to me, the more I would shut down," LeRoy said. "And even though I'm an outgoing person on the outside in public, at home I'm more introverted. And so I would retreat further and further into a shell." He eventually began battling depression, "because I didn't feel there was a way out of this."

I know these problems are hard to solve. Maybe they take years to work through. Maybe we never completely finish the process. Certainly the differences in us all will never go away, not in this lifetime or in the next. Maybe the friction those differences create won't ever fully disappear.

But while there is no cure, there is both help and hope. And we find that hope in humility.

Kimberly names humility as the first step for her and LeRoy. At one point, she had left for a retreat—to work on writing a Bible study on 1 Peter. The third chapter of Peter's letter begins with these words: "Wives, be subject to your own husbands, so that even if some do not obey the word, they may be won without a word by the conduct of their wives" (1 Peter 3:1 ESV). She'd read that chapter countless times before, but this time, given her own difficulties with LeRoy, it struck her in a new way. It broke her. When she came home, she apologized. She humbled herself.

Change didn't happen instantaneously. "My heart was so cold," LeRoy told me. It took another two years before he himself got convicted and broken and was able to come to Kimberly and apologize too. Only then could the real change, the real healing, begin.

Kimberly tells me that the secret and the real cornerstone of a great marriage is honesty through humility. Not perfection, but brokenness. A willingness to say, "I was wrong. I'm sorry. Help me."

Why do we find that so difficult?

"Do nothing out of selfish ambition or vain conceit," Paul tells the Philippian believers. "Rather, in humility value others above yourselves, not looking to your own interests but each of you to the interests of the others" (Philippians 2:3–4). We're *supposed* to be humble.

We're *supposed* to give of ourselves. And very often, we Christians can follow Paul's advice very, very well—except in our own homes. Except with the people we're supposed to love. Instead of admitting our own weaknesses, we do our best to expose theirs. We trade our brokenness for pretended perfection. We lose sight of grace for the sake of winning an argument. Our differences—our glorious, God-given differences—become flaws. Mistakes. Errors to rub out or burn away, like so much rubbish.

The longer I'm married and the more experts I talk with, the more convinced I become that we don't build a great marriage on similarities. We build them on our differences. These marriages don't depend on our strength, but on our brokenness.

Brokenness leads to humility. When we're humble, we listen better. We become more lovable. We can better see the beauty and power in our spouse, differences and all. When we're broken, we reach a better position to *need* love, and thus to *be* loved. And when we accept love, we're not just accepting a great gift; we're giving one too.

Isn't that the ultimate secret in our walk with God? We grow closest to Him when we acknowledge how much we need Him. Utter, painful honesty works best.

So why wouldn't it work the same with our husbands and wives?

Jean and I differ in some core respects. We always will. And honestly, the conflicts we have over those differences may never go away. We'll mistake them for flaws sometimes. We'll use them as weapons. Maybe we'll even try to "fix" one another, to show our spouse that our way is the *right* way.

But although we may forget that our differences are assets, God knows better. He brought us together for a reason. And He knows, better than we do ourselves, how much better we are together—not despite our differences, but because of them.

Chapter Six

MESSY LESSONS

✦

S aul and Debbie knew the fundamentals of good parenting. Everyone who knew the Colorado Springs couple would say so. They were good, middle-class people—both gainfully employed and regular churchgoers. They were in the process of raising two wonderful kids, including Cody—a smart, fun, athletic boy. Saul and Debbie did everything society tells us that good parents do. They went to every school concert, attended every soccer match. They spent time together as a family—playing games and watching cartoons, taking walks and throwing baseballs, laughing.

Or at least they laughed when it seemed appropriate. If Cody fell out of line, no one laughed. If he was rude or obnoxious at Grandma and Grandpa's house, only the occasional hissed reprimand interrupted the quiet, cold ride home. If he didn't get his homework done or came home with a poor grade, the laughter would halt abruptly, as if stopped by a kink in a garden hose. Raised voices and threats would send Cody to the dining room table, where he'd sit alone for hours, his books and papers illuminated by the chandelier overhead.

But those moments happened only rarely. Cody's parents were good parents raising a good, promising child, and they were rewarded with report cards covered in A's and B's and success on the soccer field (and even a statewide league championship). Cody was turning into everything they hoped he would—smart, driven, athletic, funny. *If only he could be better in this small area*, Saul and Debbie thought. *If only he studied a little harder in math. If only he smiled more with Grandma. If only he didn't keep asking for that dangerous skateboard. If only. If only.*

On Easter Sunday, Saul, Debbie, and the rest of the family ate dinner with Grandma and Grandpa. Cody, then twelve, seemed unusually well behaved that evening, quietly answering questions that came his way, eating all of his food. Not once did Saul need to pull Cody away to give him a stern reminder about what to say and how to say it. Not once! And on the way home, Saul even wondered whether Cody had been a little *too* quiet. He hadn't laughed as much. Not only had he not interrupted the conversation, he hadn't said much at all. Not unless someone spoke to him first.

Saul pushed the thought away. *He's just maturing,* he thought, with a swell of strangely bittersweet pride. *He's growing up. He's getting it.*

The next morning, as Saul ate his breakfast before work, Cody came downstairs in his T-shirt and shorts and walked silently to the laundry room, diving into the dryer to get some clean clothes for school.

"Good morning," Saul said.

"Morning," Cody said quietly.

"So, what's your day going to be like? Any tests?"

"Nope," Cody said.

"Great," Saul said. "Listen, before you leave, can you take out the trash for me?"

"Sure, Dad," he said.

Saul spent the next few hours immersed in work. About 11:00 a.m., he received a call from Debbie. The school had called her. Cody hadn't shown up. The secretary wanted to know if he was sick. So Debbie asked Saul.

"He might've been feeling a little sick this morning," Saul said. "He seemed awfully quiet. Maybe he just forgot to call us." *Or maybe he skipped school,* he thought darkly. *If so, we're going to make sure that never happens again.* "I'm heading home, just to make sure everything is all right," Debbie said.

Thirty minutes later, Saul's phone rang again. He noted his home number, but the sobs on the other end sounded so tight and tortured that he could barely recognize the voice.

"Debbie?" Saul asked. "What's wrong?"

He had to ask again before he could understand his wife.

"He's gone," Debbie cried. "He left a note. He ran away."

A blur of confusion and disbelief reigned over the next forty minutes. Saul raced home to find Debbie standing in the living room, still crying, holding a piece of paper in her hand.

"I'm sorry," the note began. "I love you guys, but I'm not liking my life right now." He wrote that he planned to walk to his other grandparents' house, more than a hundred miles away. He'd taken some food and a couple of changes of clothes in his backpack, along with about twenty dollars in cash. He left a small box with some things he wanted his little sister to have, just in case he didn't see her or them again.

"P.S.," he wrote. "I took out the trash."

In This Life You Will Have Trouble . . .

I hope you will never have to grapple with a crisis like that one. Saul recalls it as the worst day of his life. Debbie still struggles to talk about it. I had permission to tell this story only if I agreed to change the names.

But while the circumstances might be unique, the crisis is not. Anywhere from 1.6 to 2.8 million children run away from home every year, according to the National Runaway Safeline.[1] Most come home safely, but some do not. Some, in fact, are never found again.

Even families that never deal with a runaway child will almost certainly be confronted with a family crisis they never imagined. It could be a life-changing disaster, like a suicide attempt or an unexpected pregnancy. It could be something relatively minor that still sets off alarm bells: a D from your straight-A student; an incriminating browser history; a broken curfew; an unrepentant lie. The stories change, but the problems impact millions upon millions of families, including "good" families.

News flash: families are messy. *All* families. And the messes can feel like a volcano. In some families, they ooze over the sides and run downhill as smooth as syrup. While it's not necessarily pretty, it's steady. In others, a cork keeps the mess in. Everything looks fine from the outside, but on the inside, the pressure keeps building. And then one day, it all blows apart.

We imagine that if we do everything right, parenting won't feel so messy. If we follow all the rules, if we practice all the tips, if we listen to my knowledgeable guests on the radio every day, our families will look like those we see on television or Facebook, or those who smile at us from the walls. They'll be Mary Poppins families: practically perfect in every way. But as the guy who hosts those daily broadcasts—who hears all their wisdom firsthand—I can tell you that the messes come, even when we make all the right decisions and check all the right boxes. Why? *Because.* Because of our fallen world. Because of our fallen characters. Because we make mistakes. And because sometimes, these messes aren't mistakes at all, but lessons— God-given opportunities to pull something precious and golden out of the muck of crisis.

This feels counterintuitive to us. When we start our families, we almost immediately draft plans for our children. We may never set down a word on paper to that effect, but we carry those plans with us every day our kids are in our homes. Day by day, task by task, we see to it that they follow that plan. They fulfill it.

Mistakes don't fit in our plans. They're aberrations, flaws that can make us feel like we have to start all over again. We know what happens if we make a mistake in, say, a cookie recipe and add a cup of salt when it called for a cup of sugar. We know what happens if we skip a step in building a bicycle.

But what if our plans are filled with flaws themselves? What if God is giving us a better set of blueprints?

We hate mistakes. We hate to see them in our children, and we especially hate them in ourselves. But remember, this fallen world crumpled up and kicked away God's own plans for it long ago, and mistakes are no aberration here. We should expect them. And sometimes God may be nudging us through these mistakes—pushing us closer to His own plans for us.

The Aftermath

When Cody ran away, it was 2003. Not everyone had a cell phone stuffed in their pockets back then. Cody's parents didn't want him to have a phone until he turned sixteen anyway, so his parents couldn't call or text him. There wasn't a way to track him down unless Cody himself wanted to be found. Debbie and Saul had limited options. Saul set out on foot, trying to follow the logic of a twelve-year-old runaway and follow his steps. Debbie started heading north, along the interstate—the road that Cody would've associated with trips to Grandma and Grandpa's house. Saul and Debbie enlisted the help of friends and family. The search was on.

But Cody wasn't hiding in the neighborhood, making a terrible plea for attention. He wasn't walking as if he hoped to be found.

Saul hadn't seen a sign of the boy in ninety minutes of searching. He called Cody's name until his voice grew hoarse. Memories of his times with Cody—hiking, playing video games, watching cartoons on Saturday mornings—flashed through his mind. Was he lost? Hurt? Even in his panic, Saul wondered what his life would look like without Cody. Whether he'd ever smile again.

He came back home, his face wet with sweat and tears, ready to call 911. He saw the flashing light on the answering machine.

"Hi," the voice said, "it's Cody. I'm OK. I'm at the outlet mall in Castle Rock [a town about forty miles north of Colorado Springs]."

There was a pause.

"I want to come home now. Can someone pick me up?"

About the time Saul and Debbie read his note, Cody had already walked five miles to a fast-food joint by the interstate. There he met a man who asked Cody if he needed a ride. Cody said he did. The two took off together in a red Dodge pickup, headed north.

But then, about halfway to the grandparents' house, Cody decided to end his runaway day. He asked the man to drop him off and the man complied.

Imagine, for a moment, what sort of man would pick up a twelve-year-old boy, a runaway, in a fast-food joint. Imagine how many ways this story could've ended.

But it didn't.

A half hour after Cody's call, Saul walked into the mall food court and saw his son, backpack still slung over his shoulder, sitting with a couple of security guards. The father called the boy's name. Cody looked around and ran toward him. They cried as they hugged. Through the blur, Saul saw one of the security guards smile through a trembling lip and slowly ease away without a word.

"Let's go home," Saul said at last. "Let's go home."

The next day, Saul and Debbie took Cody to a counselor. The boy insisted he was fine now, but it'd be crazy to trust Cody's word—it being not even twenty-four hours after they'd scoured the city looking for him. He saw the counselor alone—without his parents. If he had run away because of something they did, or something they didn't do, he might be unable to say so in front of them—too scared, too shy. They waited for an hour for him and for answers.

But they got none. Cody said he didn't know why he did it. The counselor said he seemed just fine. They could sign him up for regular counseling sessions if they wanted to, but she didn't think it was necessary.

"Early adolescence is a strange time," she said. "So many chemicals surging through the body, so many conflicting emotions, so many different stressors. It can feel like you're going to explode. I guess in Cody's case, he sort of did."

To this day, that's the only explanation any of them ever received. A fluke. It happens.

But from then on, Saul and Debbie changed slightly as parents. Instead of clamping down harder on their former runaway—their natural instinct—they loosened their grip just a bit. When Cody did something well, they concentrated on praising him. When he screwed up, they tried to correct the behavior without criticizing him. They gave him a little more leeway in some of the areas they'd been so strict with before. They even let Cody buy a skateboard.

It's not as if they stopped being Cody's parents. They still wanted him to do well in school and treat his elders with respect. But in that very messy crisis, Saul and Debbie learned a beautiful, terrible lesson. They learned that their son was not just a living lump of clay to be molded, shaped, and fired in an image pleasing to God, but a gift from that very same God—a child made in His image and as worthy of not just their love and time and accumulated wisdom, but also their grace. Before that experience, they perhaps had looked at much of the time they spent with Cody as opportunities to teach, correct, and instruct. From then on, every moment they spent with their child, even as he grew into adulthood, was a celebration. Each minute was a gift in itself—because not a single one was guaranteed to exist at all.

Down and Dirty

I think Cody's family learned something about messes.

For years, I imagine Saul and Debbie tried to avoid messes

whenever possible. And when they came, they wanted to minimize them. Sweep them under the rug. When Cody was little, his parents combed his hair, washed his face, and made sure his shirt was clean whenever they went out. He wasn't allowed to splash through the mud. Heaven help him if he spilled grape juice on his shirt! And as he got older, his parents' idea of keeping him *clean* and *presentable* grew. Even as they turned their attention away from how Cody looked and concentrated on how he acted, they still focused on appearance. *Other families might be messy,* Cody's parents were trying to tell the world. *Not this one. We're good parents. We're Christian parents. We've got it together. Messes—those are for other families.*

And so maybe the pressure built, week by week. Everything looked just fine from the outside, until finally . . . BOOM.

Now they know. Messes are a part of the gig. Some families are messier than others, but the fact that they sometimes break or get a little grungy shouldn't surprise us. Each child is conceived in the messy act of sex. Our first child was born in a wash of fluid and pain. In no time at all, your little bundle of joy begins filling her diapers and spitting up all over your new cardigan. Even when you put the baby wipes away, the messes never stop. They involve fewer bodily discharges, maybe, but they never stop. Not when your kids turn five or fifteen or even sometimes thirty-five. You always have something to deal with. There's always a mess to mop up.

Even if you're fully loaded with the knowledge of the world, a PhD in parenting in hand, it still doesn't always work out. We have no guarantees. Sure, the fundamentals are important. But knowing those core fundamentals does not necessarily mean they're lived every day. And even when they are, things can still go wrong.

But if messes are unavoidable, why do so many parents fear them? We deal with dirty diapers as part of the deal . . . but misbehavior? Failure? Why do these messy moments sap our grace and turn us into dictators? Even though no parent in their right mind would trade a healthy family for a dysfunctional one, we end up doing exactly that.

Judging by our words, deeds, and choices, it sometimes seems we'd rather have a dysfunctional family that *looks* great than a messy one that's healthy.

Why? It all comes down to pressure.

First, we put it on ourselves. If we were raised by great parents, we want to follow in their footsteps, and we feel the pressure to live up to their example. If our childhoods didn't feel so hot, we want to avoid the mistakes our moms and dads made. Often we find ourselves doing a little of both. But regardless, we feel the pressure. We know how important our jobs are, and we take it very seriously (as we should).

And most of the time, we think we succeed. We think we're pretty good. You look at studies of self-evaluation forms, and you'll find that people almost always rate themselves high. They're an above-average employee or a good spouse or a curve-busting parent. Asked to grade ourselves, we tend to give ourselves A's and B's. But typically, as I found out, we score ourselves far higher than our spouses would. We give ourselves better grades than our kids would. We think we're a nine or a ten. The people who love us most might give us a six or a seven. And it's hard to hear we're a seven. So most of the time, we don't even ask.

But even more pressure comes outside our own families. It doesn't take long for the battle of the babies to start.

We track the development of our kids from the opening bell. *Is he holding his head up? Is he crawling yet? Is she talking? Is she potty trained?* We pay so much attention to those markers, not because they're important in and of themselves, but because we find ourselves in a strange, utterly meaningless competition with the family down the street who has a child about the same age as ours. Or we compete against some developmental chart we read about online or heard from a friend. We pay so much attention to these arbitrary measuring sticks that, by the time they're three, we're already enrolling our kid in Yale or resigning them to a life of crime.

It's like a pediatrician once told me: "You don't see fourteen-year-olds walking around in diapers." Yes, moms may worry about their late-blooming toddlers who just don't seem to have the knack for using a toilet. And every now and then, we have reason to worry. But for the most part, these kids get it. It may take a while, but they get it. "Don't sweat the small stuff," this pediatrician said. And you have to know what the small stuff is. Being potty trained by the age of one isn't necessarily a big deal.

But even though pediatricians don't worry, moms and dads still use the measuring stick. If their child sits on the upper end of the developmental curve, you can bet that the parents will let everyone close to them know. If kids fall on the lower end of the curve, parents don't just worry. They feel *embarrassed*. They feel *ashamed* that their child isn't getting it as quickly as the other children they know. They're stressed that their son or daughter—and by extension, the whole family—will be targets of malicious gossip. "Little Tommy Jenkins is three and a half, and he's still not potty trained. Why, my Meggie Sue was flushing the potty—the full-size adult one, mind you, not the plastic one—when she was eighteen months old!"

And so it begins. All the pressure. All the expectations. "*My* kid's on the honor roll." "*My* kid's on varsity." "*My* kid's going to Stanford. What's *your* kid done lately?"

The pressures, both internal and external, can be tremendous. And that fear of failure, that fear of mess, is particularly strong in Christians.

Dancing with Expectations

These pressures run directly counter to who we're supposed to be and the grace we've been given. Within the Christian community, we're deathly afraid to project imperfection. Many of us Christians work very hard to hide our doubts and fears and insecurities. We learn a way of talking. We learn a way of behaving. We learn a way of *hiding*. And that extends to our families.

Funny that we don't see many families hiding in the Bible. Scripture is so full of messy families that it can be hard to find a good one. We don't find Brady families in the Bible. Some of them are downright dysfunctional. It's not healthy for a mom to scheme with her favorite son to pull a fast one on Dad, like Rebekah and Jacob did. If you're raising a family where your sons sell one of their own into slavery, you've got some serious problems.

Even the Bible's most famous family wasn't perfect. Most of us, even in our worst parenting moments, wouldn't forget to take our kid home after a trip to the big city, would we? But that's what Mary and Joseph did with Jesus in Jerusalem, right when he was the same age as Saul's son Cody.

The Bible doesn't shrink away from the world's messes. The Bible deals with reality.

I go back again and again to the example set by David. He was far from perfect. He sinned—and sometimes in a big way. But he knew who he was. He knew his inadequacies. And despite all his flaws, the Bible tells us that God loved him. That he was a man after God's own heart (see 1 Samuel 13:14).

What a mystery that line is, given David's flaws and checkered past. *Really? A man after God's own heart?* But here's what I take from that. David lived a bold life. An honest life. A *messy* life. He didn't live in fear. He didn't live trying to vindicate the expectations of others. When he felt joyful, he shouted. When he was in anguish, he cried. When he felt anxious or depressed, he didn't hide it: He wrote searing, raw psalms about it.

When the ark of the covenant came to Jerusalem, David danced before the Lord, which horrified his wife, Michal (see 2 Samuel 6:14–16). *Doesn't he know what people must think of him?* I imagine her thinking. *Has he no shame? Doesn't he know that he's the king?* "How the king of Israel has distinguished himself today, going around half-naked in full view of the slave girls of his servants as any vulgar fellow would!" she sarcastically says in 2 Samuel 6:20.

David danced before the Lord, the Bible says—half-naked. He

hid nothing, inside or out. And Michal? Her shame and her worry over other people's expectations feel . . . very familiar. She might as well be the patron saint for Christian family dysfunction.

David danced. He modeled for us the joy we should feel in God, the joy we should show our families. But the world steals from us our sense of joy because we're so locked down. We're so unable to live in the moment. It's almost as if, in modern Christianity, we're discouraged from feeling real joy. We can't show real, soul-crushing sadness. We're encouraged to be pleasant—to show up at church and smile and make polite conversation. When someone asks how we are, we say, "Good. And you?" even if we're dying inside. We encourage our children to say please and thank you and to sit still and be quiet and never, ever run or jump in the sanctuary.

Don't get me wrong. Kids shouldn't run roughshod during the message or shout during the Lord's Prayer. But sometimes, in our efforts to hide our true feelings and to stifle those of our children, we discourage any feeling at all—well, unless you count guilt as a feeling. We're plenty good about feeling bad about what we have or haven't done. We're very adept at making our kids feel guilty.

No wonder our kids are saying, "That's not for me." No wonder they're leaving the faith. "I've got one life," they're saying. "I don't want to feel guilty all the time."

Again, I'm not arguing that we don't have things to feel guilty about. I'm not trying to remove the passion of the Holy Spirit. What I'm talking about is being honest—about understanding our foibles as human beings, like David did. To not just live large, but to learn in the course of that living, and to have the capacity to say, "God, forgive me!" at the deepest level of our hearts. There weren't two Bathshebas; there was one. David learned from his terrible failures. He mourned them . . . and then he moved on. The question for us is, can we give ourselves the grace to learn from our own failures? Can we grant our kids the same sort of grace?

This life is going to pull us downward. Paul writes about it regularly.

"We see only a reflection as in a mirror," he says in 1 Corinthians 13:12. He talks about a "thorn in my flesh" in 2 Corinthians 12:7. "I do not understand what I do," he writes in Romans 7:15. "For what I want to do I do not do, but what I hate I do." In Acts 14:22, Paul says "we must go through many hardships to enter the kingdom of God." Jesus spoke about it at length too. "The thief comes only to steal and kill and destroy," we read in John 10:10. Sin is a reality. Messes, sometimes big messes, are inescapable. Living in the flesh, living in this life—encountering messes is part of what's going to happen to us.

But what does Jesus say in the very next sentence in John 10? "I have come that they may have life, and *have it to the full.*"*

There it is again. That sense of joy in the midst of the mess. That sense of hope in a fallen world. That freedom to dance.

How do we give our children that freedom to dance while guiding them toward sanctification? How do we encourage joy while still encouraging good behavior and all the lessons we know they'll need as they grow?

We've been given a deceptively simple answer: We need to relax a little. We need to stop worrying so much about other people's expectations and see our kids a little more like God sees them. Most importantly, we need to give our kids the grace to make mistakes, to fail sometimes and learn from those failures.

But as easy as it is to say, it can be awfully difficult to do.

Fostering Family

As I write this in 2016, the Daly family is two kids bigger. We have a pair of foster children with us, ages three and five. We can't use their real names, but we'll call them John and Jerilee. We're watching them while their mother dealt with some legal issues and got her life back on track.

---

* Emphasis mine.

We were happy to do it, though Jean was the one who really stepped up. The rest of us were reluctant. But these kids needed a little stability in their lives, even though in the short term, the learning curve for everyone can be pretty steep. The kids coming in have to acclimate to a new mom, a new dad, new siblings, and lots of new ways of doing things. They could be struggling with different expectations and different habits. It can be bewildering. As a former foster kid myself, I know what it's like.

But it's no stroll in the shade for the hosting family either. Welcoming new brothers and sisters into your home is always a challenge, even when they're tiny blank slates brought straight from the delivery room. But foster children—they're already becoming, or have become, their own people. Many come from very difficult home lives that have left serious scars on their psyches. They may have behavioral difficulties or trust issues. While fostering kids is a wonderful, beautiful way to speak into someone's life and can be deeply rewarding for everyone involved, each foster situation comes with challenges. Each has its own messes, and foster families expect them.

So when we opened our family to Jerilee and John, it wasn't a decision any of us took lightly. We knew these kids had already experienced some pretty rough times. They came from a background different from the one we were trying to provide for Trent and Troy. In some ways, it was a different world. And we were determined to be the best parents we could be for these children, for however long we had them.

Honestly, I'm not nearly as good as Jean is with our foster kids. I'm probably not as attentive as I could or should be—a little weird, given my background. But Jean is amazing with these kids. She really is. She plays games with them, reads them to sleep at night, and does everything in her power to make sure they're experiencing a loving, safe home. If they spill something or make a mistake, she's very understanding. Instead of getting angry, she'll let it pass with a smile and a laugh. Jean has an incredible capacity to serve those children. She's the picture of grace.

I try to follow her example as much as I can. We want to give these kids as much comfort and security as we can while they're here. I don't want to overspiritualize this, but we try to model Jesus for them. To show them what His love and grace look like, hoping to make a difference in their lives. Hoping they'll be able to carry a hint of God's reflection throughout the rest of their lives.

But while we hope these foster kids are watching us and learning, maybe we forgot that Trent and Troy were watching and learning too. One day, when they thought Jean and I were out of earshot, we heard them talking to one another.

"It'd be awesome if Mom and Dad treated us the way they do those foster kids," they said.

BOOM.

We Christians understand grace. We know its significance better than anybody. And we can be so good in showering that grace on other people. The poor. The suffering. The widows. The foster kids. I know Christians who have given jobs to convicted killers and have opened their homes to the homeless. According to a study by Connected to Give, the more religious a person is, the more likely she is to give to charity.[2] Other sources say that individuals gave nearly $265 billion to charitable causes in 2015, a third of that going to religious organizations.[3] According to Gallup, nearly two-thirds of Americans volunteered in 2014, with researchers finding that "Christians are more likely than those with no religious affiliation to report that they made donations and volunteered time."[4] Even atheists see how dedicated we Christians are to showing God's love and mercy in important, pragmatic ways. "For all of the faults in theology, Christians have a lock on charity work," reads a post from Minnesota Atheists.[5]

But if charity begins at home, why do we sometimes struggle to show charity in our *own* homes, with the people closest to us? We understand that the world is a messy place, and we'll wade into that world with both feet and a smile on our face. But if we see a messy bedroom, we come down like a brick house.

We save our grace for outsiders. We reserve our tolerance for those who "need" it. But in Christian families, more often than not, we operate far more on an expectation/reward cycle. We're big on "if you act right, you'll get rewarded, but if you behave inappropriately, you'll be penalized." It's as if we imagine we're raising lab rats, not children of God: solve the maze, get a pellet; take a wrong turn, get a shock.

It's so different from what God does with us, isn't it? He doesn't ask us to be perfect. He expects the mess. He knows we're messy people. "I want you to live a life that's reflective of My character," he tells us. "But I'm not judging you on your behavior. I've already got it covered. You're Mine not because of what you've done, but what I've done for you."

God tells us He loves us. And as we grow to understand that love more and more, we want to follow His example more and more. It doesn't work the other way—that God says if we'll behave, He'll love us. But sometimes that's what we convey to our children, isn't it? We ask them for their obedience, for their unwavering commitment to us and our rules, for their perfection. And we forget that the messes they sometimes make are part of growing up. They're messy because they're born messy, and they're still learning. And so are we.

God Is the Real Artist

I understand we need to discipline our children. I understand we need to give them the tools to become happy, successful men and women, and we can't do that by accepting and validating every word and action.

But what we often do as parents goes beyond the realm of correction. It falls into the realm of *re-creation*. We imagine these children as lumps of clay to be molded into whatever shape we see fit, and that shape often looks a lot like us. We forget that God had something in mind for our children before we ever set eyes on them. "For you created my inmost being," we read in Psalm 139:13–14. "You knit me together in my mother's womb. I praise you because I am fearfully and wonderfully made; your works are wonderful, I know that full well."

Michelangelo reportedly once said of one of his statues, "I saw the angel in the marble and carved until I set him free."[6] When you read his philosophy of artwork, the great Renaissance artist modestly believed that his talent stemmed not from taking a hunk of nothing—a block of marble, a lump of clay—and turning it into *something*. He saw *something*, and something beautiful, already within. "Every block of stone has a statue inside it," he also reportedly said, "and it is the task of the sculptor to discover it."[7]

Maybe that's the primary job of moms and dads too. We're given these . . . things, these little children who begin their lives squalling and screaming. And over the next eighteen or twenty-two or twenty-five years, we work on them, honing them and molding them, bringing out the beauty and wonder and greatness that God gave them. It's not our job as parents to mold and carve and beat our children into a shape more pleasing to *us*. Even though we have a huge influence on who our children become, we shouldn't use our rules and expectations to make someone in our own image. God made our children, and He made them beautiful. We need to train them in the wisdom of the Lord. Provide boundaries. But we also need to avoid messing them up too much!

As any artist knows, it's still hard work. It's messy work. Go into any painter's studio, and you'll likely see splotches of paint on the walls and floors. Go into a sculptor's workshop, and you'll see dirt and grit and hunks of rock everywhere. Sit with a band at practice, and you'll hear caterwauling notes. Look over a writer's shoulder, and watch how many words he deletes for every word he keeps.

Mess. It's part of creation. It's part of life. Our task as parents isn't to avoid it; it's to accept it. Sometimes even celebrate it. Because out of the mess, something beautiful can come.

PART THREE

Troubleshooting

Chapter Seven

THE BLAME GAME

✦

C raig was the life of the party.

Even though most of Jean's family has a history of depression, Jean's brother seemed like the last person who'd try to hurt himself. Sure, we knew he'd had some setbacks lately. His business in Orange County, California, had been struggling. But whenever I saw him, he still had that same fun-loving spirit, still felt like that same guy who'd do anything to help you out. He never showed any desperation.

But then Craig went missing. And as Jean and I waited for word, we worried. We prayed. We prepared for the worst.

It was obviously a difficult, stressful day, made more awkward by the fact that we had houseguests. Some of Jean's friends from high school were moving to the area, and they were staying with us for a couple of weeks while they looked for a house. Both of them knew not only Jean but Craig as well; they were grappling with the crisis along with us. And while I think Jean found some comfort in their company, it was admittedly a little awkward for me. I didn't know them that well. But together, we dealt with the uncertainty as best we could. It was a long, terrible day—and it was about to get worse.

The call came in late that night—nearly midnight—as Jean and I were getting ready for bed.

Craig had killed himself.

Do I even need to describe how we felt in that moment? The pain, the overwhelming sadness, the anger directed at ourselves that we could have, or should have, done more? It felt like I'd been punched in the gut. I can't even begin to imagine how Jean felt. Her brother was gone.

In moments like these, the world stops spinning for a moment. Everything freezes as the anguish washes over you like a tide, covering you in grief. You just want to stop. You want to bury yourself in your emotions until you can make some sense of it all, until you can face the world again.

But the world doesn't allow for that. Life goes on. We make decisions in those moments that can impact us profoundly and scar us deeply. And in the blur of the moment, even those critical decisions can become blurred. Reality itself can get confused.

To this day, Jean and I do not have the same memories of what happened that night, but we do know we miscommunicated. Chalk it up to grief. The late hour. My not thinking clearly. Her being overwhelmed with emotion. Whatever the reason, this family tragedy was about to take a strange, frustrating turn.

Tragedy Compounded

My own recollection feels, frankly, crystal clear—or so it seems to me. Jean and I learned about the horror together. And in that moment, we had a decision to make: Should we tell our houseguests?

I remember snapping into action mode—me, that roll-with-the-punches guy, the fix-it guy, the guy who can deal with life's hardships without breaking a sweat. And to me, the thing that made the most sense was for us to stay upstairs and talk in our bedroom. The news could wait.

Tell them tomorrow, I thought. *Why open all this up right now with them? It'll be there tomorrow. Why not talk with them in the morning, once you've had a chance to cry into my heart, into my chest? Let's grieve together, you and I.*

But Jean needs to process these things more openly than I do. That door of mine that Jean says is always shut? Hers was open that night. Plus, she couldn't just keep the news from these longtime family friends. She wanted them to know. She intended to go tell them. And of course, I understood. I understood the need to tell her friends. But I figured that, when it came time to truly grieve and process, we'd do it together in private. I certainly didn't feel comfortable unpacking this horrifically personal moment with people I considered nearly strangers. *She'll tell them the bad news*, I thought. *She'll come to bed, and we can process it together.* In fact, I *knew* she was coming back. In my recollection of that evening, she *told* me that was exactly what she was going to do.

But Jean's own memories tell her something very different.

We still don't agree as to even *why* she went downstairs. She remembers the phone ringing. It was Craig's wife. She and Jean were very close and talked often, especially during this critical time. While on the phone, Craig's wife said, "Oh no, there's a police officer at the door." She told Jean she would call her back and hung up the phone. As she heard the click, Jean's heart sank. She tried convincing herself of some other reason for a police officer to come to the door, but deep down, she knew Craig was gone.

Jean recalls *not* wanting to wake her friends. She remembers going downstairs and waiting for the phone to ring again. And when it did ring, her worst fears were realized. Jean remembers sobbing on the phone with Craig's wife. After a long while, they hung up.

Jean recalls staying downstairs, alone and sobbing, wondering why I wasn't coming to comfort her. She remembers crying so loudly that one of her friends—the one perhaps closest to Craig—heard her.

In those critical moments, I thought she'd tell them and *come back*; she thought I'd *come down*.

The clock ran on. We waited for each other—me, alone, in my pajamas in bed; she, sobbing, with her friend downstairs. For two hours we waited. And by the time she did come upstairs, she wasn't just grieving over the loss of her brother; she had a fresh wound.

Her perspective: *In that moment when I needed you the most, you weren't there.*

My perspective: *In that moment when I wanted to be there for you, you walked away. You went to talk with your friends from high school instead of being with me.*

To this day, that's probably one of the greatest disappointments Jean has in our relationship. That night, and in the months to come, Jean felt I locked away the part of me that empathizes with her pain. It's an issue we couldn't even talk about for a decade. The pain was too present. The anger was too close to the surface.

If we had a do-over, we'd take it. I'd come down. Or she'd come up. Maybe we'd meet on the stairs and hold each other there. At the very least, we'd make sure we'd be on the same page. I would take the time to come alongside and to understand her pain.

But we don't get do-overs in this life. There are no mulligans, no save screens. The decisions we make we have to keep and deal with somehow. We either make peace with the situation somehow, forgive, and move on . . . or we sink into judgment. Hurt. Anger.

We blame.

For years, Jean and I have blamed each other for what happened that night. Sometimes when we feel stressed or angry, we'll rehash that memory—not to find resolution, but to use it as ammunition for whatever we're discussing. More often, it's simply there, under the surface. That wordless blame. That shadowy finger pointing in accusation. *This is your fault.*

Even now, when I think about that evening, I'm *sure* she said she'd be right back. Ask Jean, and she'd be *positive* she said no such thing. If we had a record of that evening, we could go to the instant replay, like an NFL referee, and figure out who said what—who's right and who's mistaken. But there's no hope of that in this life. The pain of that moment—and the blame—is something we've come to live with. And maybe we always will. It's so tender, so tough, that we don't adequately talk about it. We've never put it to rest.

Pointing Fingers

It's been said there are only two certain things in life: death and taxes. I think I'd add a third: blame. Everybody does it. When we hurt, we want to blame someone. We want to hold someone responsible. "It's *your* fault," we say. "This happened because of *you*."

Laying blame isn't always bad. If someone slugs you in the face or steals your car, you want to know who did it. Prisons are full of people who are taking the blame for something, and I'd say most of them deserve to be there. As their mothers might say, they have only themselves to blame.

Even in a family, it's sometimes necessary to lay the blame at someone's feet. If Tommy puts the cat in the dryer, you've got to waggle your finger at Tommy and make sure it doesn't happen again. If your son ditches class or your daughter drinks a beer, you have to correct that behavior. Those situations did not "just happen"; it's someone's fault. And when someone's obviously at fault, they need to be called on it and the behavior corrected. That's not being judgmental; that's just being a good parent. And that goes for our relationship with our spouses too. When we act like jerks, who else is more likely to tell us that?

When Jean and I get in a heated discussion about the boys, she'll sometimes turn to me and say, "You know, you think you're perfect, Jim. But you're really not. You're not the perfect parent." And you know what? She's right—and right to tell me. Sometimes I can give myself a better grade than I deserve. Sometimes I *need* that little arrow of doubt to prick my perception of perfection.

But so often in our families, blame takes on strange, even frightening dimensions. We stop looking at blame as the first step toward correction and think of it as the last. We'd rather punish the wrongdoer than fix the wrongdoing. We use our imperfections as excuses to treat each other terribly rather than using the grace of God to encourage one another.

We sometimes call it "the blame game," and in some ways, we really do turn it into a game. It becomes a mean-spirited round of Monopoly, where the object is to pound your opponents into emotional bankruptcy. To shame them. Break them. To hurt them like they hurt you. When the blame game really starts cranking, it's not so much about making ourselves *better* as making our opponents—our spouses, our children—feel *worse*. We find no free parking here, no get-out-of-jail-free card. When we play this game, we play it together in a prison of our own making.

Even when we nail down the fundamentals—we talk and laugh and obey the Golden Rule—our inclination to blame never goes away. We can't shake it. When families struggle, it seems as though blame is often a huge component.

Don't believe me? Just look at the stories in this book.

In chapter 1, I told you about my friend and his wife, Kathy, who discovered their son had been looking at porn. "How could we let this happen?" Kathy said. Then she pointed the finger of blame to her husband. "How could *you* let this happen?"

I told you about Casey and Doug, who were faced with the unexpected pregnancy of their daughter. What was the first thing Casey's own father said to her? "We're so disappointed in you." *This is your fault*, he was saying. *I blame you*. Even if she was right—and she was—the added kick was painful, not helpful.

Practically every story in this book has a kernel of blame at its source. We just can't get away from it. We can't escape blame in family life. It's as pervasive an influence in our homes as love and affection are. When we get wrapped up in perfection, when we feel preoccupied with what our family *should* be, we need to figure out what went wrong when it falls short. Blame is the inevitable offshoot.

Families are natural breeding grounds for blame. It begins with Mom and Dad blaming each other for their faults and differences. Kids learn to lay blame from the moment they're first denied that cookie before dinner. Can't see that movie? Blame Dad. Don't like dinner? Blame Mom. We have so much control and influence in our children's lives that we're bound to make our children miserable every now and then. It's part of the gig.

But we sometimes lose sight of the fact that we also, perhaps unintentionally at times, blame our children for making *our* lives more difficult. We blame them when they wake up squalling at two in the morning and just won't stop. We blame them when they just can't get the hang of the potty. We sometimes get frustrated because our lives without children looks so glamorous compared to the lives we now have as parents. We throw up our hands in exasperation at their grades, knowing it's going to force *us* to ride roughshod over them until they improve. We groan and roll our eyes when they spill the milk *again*.

That last one hits home for me. When the kids were younger, it seemed like every other morning, there'd be a mess of milk on the floor. I'd lash out. Sometimes I'd crack a joke no one laughed at: "Wow, look. Troy spilled milk *again*." I'd ask him just when he'd learn to keep the milk in the glass, like normal people. And as I'd dig at him, the blame would be unmistakable. *You failed me*, I was saying underneath my heavy sighs and rolling eyes. *You're either too careless or too dumb to do what most people are able to do by the time they're four years old.*

Then one day, Troy turned to me and said, "But, Dad, it's only milk." And you know what? He was absolutely right. Spilling milk isn't a moral failing. It's not a sign of feeblemindedness. It's not as if the milk was going to burn through the floor, or that buying another half gallon a day earlier than we would have was going to bankrupt us. My attitude had nothing at all to do with my trying to correct Troy's behavior; it had everything to do with me. My need to blame him for another minor wrench in the day, my annoyance at having to deal with yet another mess.

It happens to all of us. But it's just spilled milk. We shouldn't cry about it. We cry and whine about a great many things in our lives that aren't worth the tears. We blame, when it's just not worth it.

We have to be careful to catch ourselves when we blame our kids unfairly or out of proportion to what they've done. Sometimes the blame we lay at our children's feet can leave painful, lifelong wounds.

Several years ago, Drs. Tom and Beverly Rodgers joined guest host Frank Pastore on the Focus on the Family broadcast. Both came from dysfunctional homes that left them deeply scarred. Beverly's mother had abused her emotionally, and Beverly talked about it on the show.

"Things were said to me, Frank, like, '*You're no good. You'll never amount to anything. I wish you hadn't been born.* I'm a single mom with four kids, so nobody wants me.'"

She told Frank that her mother told her she had wished she'd been able to abort her. And Frank, the host, admitted his own mother had told him the same thing: "I wish I had aborted you."

"I'm fifty-one years old," Frank said. "I mean, I . . . I still teared up just remembering that."

As parents, most of us may read this and wonder what monstrous mothers would ever say such a thing to a child. It seems unthinkable. We'd *never* say such things to our own children. But even if we'd never go so far, strange, demeaning words can still come out of our mouths when we grow angry and frustrated. We sometimes say unthinkable things, things we don't even believe. When we grow too invested in the blame game, we'll say almost anything to win. We'll say almost anything to get a rise out of someone. But what we say, whether we mean it or not, leaves scars.

No—more than scars. Open wounds.

Tom and Beverly say they're still dealing with the baggage from their dysfunctional families. Seemingly unrelated events can trigger waves of almost uncontrollable anger or sadness in them. It's why they wrote the book that brought them to the broadcast: *Becoming a Family That Heals.*[1]

"We wrote the book because basically we wanted people to know that you can come from a really poor family, a real unhealthy family, and raise good kids," Beverly says. "Not without making mistakes.

We're all gonna make mistakes. But . . . there is hope that you don't have to feel like raising your kids is doomed."

Even when we're honestly trying to *correct* our children, blame can turn unhealthy very, very quickly. Unhealthy blame, particularly when we turn it on our children, quickly turns into tearing someone down. It becomes an exercise in shame and condemnation, two of the most devastating and dangerous weapons in our arsenal. We think blame will make our kids better somehow. We'll shame them into treating their brothers and sisters better. We'll demean them for the D they got in algebra. We'll make them feel so bad that they'll never spill milk again. We end up believing that something good can come out of someone feeling bad.

We're going for spiritual conviction. What we wind up doing is throwing our loved ones into an emotional prison.

It goes back to our obsession with perfection. We want things to be perfect, and when they're not, we need to blame someone. Every family plays this game. The Dalys do it too.

I know the satisfaction of "winning" the game. When I come home and find chaos in the house—the kids are arguing, the place is a mess, the whole house feels like it's about to explode—my first response is to blame someone. After all, *I* wasn't there. It's not *my* fault that dishes are all over the kitchen. I didn't have anything to do with whatever Trent and Troy are yelling about. So I turn to Jean. "What's going on here?" I ask. But my tone says something else: *You failed, Jean. You really fell down on the job this time.* It's as though I blame Jean for having lost control of the household.

It's not a healthy response. But I doubt I'm all that unusual. When something goes wrong, we tend to look outside of ourselves to find out what happened and, more importantly, who did it. We look for someone to blame. And maybe my personality type makes me particularly susceptible. I like winning. I like to be right. When I play almost any game, I play to win, and that includes the blame game.

So the question is, how can we respond in a healthier way? How can I, instead of coming home and accusing Jean of allowing chaos to take over the household, walk in with a more open heart? How can we all learn to shelve that unneeded blame and restore a sense of grace and love?

How to Quit the Game

Restoring this sense of grace and love isn't as easy as we'd like it to be. But following a few principles can help us find a way forward.

Listen

When most of us start playing the blame game, we want to roll first. We're aggrieved. We're angry. We have plenty to say, and we're going to say it all, right then. We open the conversation. We want the last word. And we'll get in as many digs as we can and shout as much as we can along the way.

If we work at it, most of us can anticipate when we're in danger of diving into the blame game. We enter dangerous territory when we play the whole argument in our heads beforehand, or when we start thinking of soliloquies, of speeches that'll leave no room for rebuttal. (And if they try, we have our counterarguments all planned.)

But I believe I'm at my best as a husband and as a father when I don't come in with my arguments blazing. I'm better when I try to *help*, not when I try to *win*.

Trent struggled in school last year, despite his intelligence. At times I think he's the smartest one in the whole family, and his test scores back that up. But like many teens, motivation has been an issue. From September to May, his grades became an almost constant point of friction in the family, a constant source of blame. And there was plenty to go around.

Technically, of course, some of that blame fixing was justified. It really was Trent's own fault. And I doubt there was ever a time when, at least from Jean's and my perspective, that our constructive arguments were ever about winning the blame game. Both of us were simply trying to get him to do his homework, to study harder, to take the steps we all knew he *needed* to take to succeed.

But nothing seemed to work. We grew more frustrated. Our "encouragement" grew more pointed, which exasperated Trent all the more. Jean would blame me for not being hard enough on Trent; I blamed Jean for being *too* hard. Fingers got pointed everywhere. The emotional temperature of the house kept rising.

But then one night, near the end of the school year, I walked into Trent's room to talk. I had no speech planned. I didn't want to argue. I just wanted to talk. More importantly, I wanted to listen.

"What's happening? What's going on with your grades?"

Even questions can carry the baggage of blame. It's easy to imagine those words sounding more like an accusation than an honest query. But I really wanted to know. I really wanted to hear from him. And so I kept my tone calm and low.

So often, when we play the blame game—when we're trying to win instead of trying to help—everything we say can raise the hackles of the person we're talking to. When we go on the offensive, our spouses or kids automatically get defensive, and who could blame them? But when we walk into a conversation with open hands, a smile, and a willingness to listen, the defenses come down a bit. The heat diminishes. A confrontation becomes a conversation.

This wasn't the first talk I'd had with Trent about his grades, and I doubt it'll be the last. But this night, I didn't come to tell Trent what he should do. I wanted to listen to him. I wanted to hear his side of the story. I wanted him to open up to me.

And he did.

Be Honest

"What's happening?" I asked him.

"I don't know," he said softly. "I sit down to study, and I mean to do it. But then I get distracted. I can't concentrate. I start thinking about all the other things I could be doing."

"I know what I need to do," Trent said. "I know I need to study. But I can't discipline myself to do it."

So began a good conversation, one of the best Trent and I have ever had about his grades. It didn't necessarily solve anything, but the tension we'd all felt had, for the moment, evaporated. All the venom drained away. For the first time in a while, we began talking *with* each other about a really important issue, not just talking *at* each other, or over each other.

I'd like to think my attitude going in served as a catalyst for the conversation going as well as it did. But our talk still would've fallen flat if not for Trent's disarming honesty.

He didn't try to blame his teachers or the school. He didn't try to blame Jean or me for being too tough or not understanding enough. He blamed himself. He looked at the issue with honesty and clarity, and he knew the fault ultimately landed on him.

This sort of honest self-reflection is hard for most of us. When we lay blame, we almost always lay it on other people. We all see ourselves as the heroes in our own stories, and heroes don't make a lot of mistakes. It seems like whenever we argue—especially whenever we launch into the blame game—our first assumption, almost always, is that we're *right*. And it's up to us to show our spouse or our kids or the whole world just how right we are.

The Bible tells us that's hypocrisy, plain and simple.

"How can you say to your brother, 'Let me take the speck out of your eye,' when all the time there is a plank in your own eye?" Jesus tells us. "You hypocrite, first take the plank out of your own eye, and then you will see clearly to remove the speck from your brother's eye" (Matthew 7:4–5).

Plenty of husbands, wives, sons, and daughters are walking around with planks in their eyes, maybe whole trees.

When she was a guest on our broadcast some years ago, Jill Savage told our audience about how often she would blame her husband for what ailed their marriage and family. She pointed out his failings early and often. And then one day as she worked on a Bible study, she came to this very passage—the brother with the speck in his eye. And she saw something very different written in her Bible in that moment: Instead of "brother," she saw "husband."

"I know there's no version of the Bible that says 'husband,' but I swear, God changed those words on the page for me that day," she said. "And honestly, He took the plank that was in my own eye and hit me over the head with it." That moment was the first step in Jill and her husband healing their rocky relationship.

That ability to look at yourself honestly, even painfully, can do much to stop the blame game before it starts. When I think about the most critical lessons that parents can teach their children, this would be right up there with the Golden Rule. You teach your children how to treat other people; then, right alongside, you teach them how to look into their own hearts.

Truth is so critical to all our relationships. I go back to Jesus again, the ultimate Truth. What did He tell Pontius Pilate when he asked Him if He was king of the Jews? Jesus could've said, "Yes, and I've come to save the world." That in itself was true, and it would've been a powerful answer. But He said no such thing. Instead, He replied, "You say that I am a king. In fact, the reason I was born and came into the world is to testify to the truth. Everyone on the side of truth listens to me" (John 18:37).

The truth. He's the author of truth. He *is* truth. When I read the Bible, I see nothing *but* truth—even painful, embarrassing truth. The people we read about in the Scriptures aren't airbrushed, Facebook versions of themselves, showing only their best sides. They're full of faults. The lessons we learn in the Scriptures can be hard or politically incorrect. We may not want to see the truth in them. Sometimes it feels easier if we don't. But God doesn't hide the truth. It's always there. Sure, we sometimes bury it—through denial, through our own vanity, through our own weaknesses and addictions. We throw furniture on the truth or lock it in a closet. But God doesn't let us bury the truth so deeply that we can't find it.

We Christians are people raised in truth, and people of truth need to be truthful people. That starts with our own hearts. To look at them with as clear an eye and with as much clarity of mind as we can muster. We must see the planks.

In the gospel of John, Jesus tells us "the truth will set you free" (John 8:32). Jesus was talking about His truth, of course—who He was and what He came to do. But that verse is meaningful for us in this context too. If we know the truth in our own lives—what really happened to set the blame game in motion—and if we're willing to see the truth for what it is, a lot of the unproductive blame we lay at the feet of others will go away.

But *knowing* the truth can be a tricky matter in itself. That terrible night of Craig's suicide provides proof. Both Jean and I believe we know what happened, but at least one of us is wrong. Maybe both of us. And even when we *think* we know the truth, the truth can feel . . . squishy.

When that happens, there's really only one thing to do.

Laugh

Want to know another source of friction in the Daly household, another reservoir of blame? Milkshakes.

I've already told you about the soft spot I have for them, how my mom would bring me a shake home from work and leave it in the fridge, and I'd eat it for breakfast the next morning. For me, milkshakes are more than a sweet, cool treat; they're comfort food. They just whisper—in their icy, smooth tone—*family*. Even when my mom wasn't around all the time, the shakes she brought reminded me of how much she loved me.

Well, guess what? Now I'm the working adult who's not at home as much as I'd like. Monday through Friday, I'm at the office for most of the day. I have just a few hours in the evenings to spend with my kids most weeknights. And when their bedtimes came earlier years ago, that time was even more precious. I'd get home, and before I knew it, the kids were trundling off to bed.

So the weekends became Dad time: Jean would often stay home while the boys and I went out and did something in the morning. We'd typically grab lunch afterward, and naturally, I'd let them order a milkshake. Even though I've stopped drinking them, no reason my boys can't enjoy a bit of sugary family goodness.

But when Jean thinks milkshake, she doesn't think family; she thinks calories. Sugar. Rotting teeth. Hyperactivity. *Good parents don't let their kids get milkshakes every weekend*, she reasons. So she'd get on my case. "The kids need to eat healthier," she'd tell me. The boys weren't eating well, and Jean thought it was *all my fault*. She'd *never* allow them to eat what I let them eat.

But I had no intention of taking all that blame on my shoulders without proof. So over the course of a few weeks or so, I kept a tally of how Jean and the boys ate when I wasn't around. If I worked late, I'd give Jean a call and ask what they'd had for dinner.

"Oh, we just picked up some fast food," she'd say.

"*Again?*" I'd retort in mock amazement.

By the end of the period, the results were in. I was, by far, the more nutritionally responsible parent. Not that Jean believed me. To this day, she believes that I'm *far* worse about letting the boys have sugar. I know better, of course. But what can we do about it? Laugh about it. It's a running joke in our family—and a little nudge for both of us to watch what we and our kids eat.

Now, laughter isn't a cure-all. We can feel too strongly to laugh about certain issues. The emotions can feel too raw. The blame can run too deep. But very often, laughter can move us out of that blame game where no one wins and into a realm where . . . well, still no one wins, but no one cares that much. And that's a much better place to be.

Be Gracious; Be Humble

When Jesus walked the earth, He found plenty wrong with it. Wrong with us. If anyone had the right to condemn us or shame us, Jesus did. But you rarely see Him shaming anybody. He's very direct, but when He brings out the heavy rhetorical guns—comparing the Pharisees to a "brood of vipers," for instance (Matthew 23:33)—it wasn't because of the sins they've committed, but because of their hypocrisy and legalism. He didn't hammer them for what they'd done, but for what they pretended to be—perfect. But when Jesus confronted a sinner, we see a very different Messiah—a gentle, forgiving Savior. He comforts, directs, protects, and tells them to "go now and leave your life of sin" (John 8:11). There's no blame there. He simply points them—points us—in a better direction.

As spouses and as parents, I wonder if we've really learned from Jesus' example. We fall into our blame game, our shaming game, and it drives people away from us. Who wants to be around *that*? Nobody. If you have a boss who shames you, you'll find another job. If you have a friend who regularly makes you feel like dirt, you'll likely find another friend. Why would our children react any differently when we shame them? What child would not feel angry and hurt?

Sometimes, we parents forget that our children are works in progress. We forget that they're on an emotional and spiritual journey, just like we are—and they're years behind us on that journey. They don't have it figured out yet. And guess what? *We don't either.*

That's important to remember. When we talk with our kids and lay down the blame, we forget. Yes, maybe we're ahead of where they are. Sure, we might have some big things managed. But none of us have it all figured out.

Why, then, do we wrap ourselves in a cloak of perfection for the benefit of our kids? We don't want our kids to ever call our judgment into question, and so we invoke—or, to our kids, seem to invoke—a rule of parental infallibility: *We don't make mistakes. Father knows best. Mother's always right.*

That, in itself, can cause problems, but when we pair it with blame, it can be downright corrosive. Because when we lay blame in a shaming and demeaning manner, we're not just telling them they're bad: We're telling them they're *worse* human beings than we are. That we're *better* than they are. Implicit in any game is the concept of keeping score, and we constantly look for points in the blame game. Again, we want to win.

But Jesus taught us that sometimes to win, we have to lose. We have to give our children our humanness, in an age-appropriate way. Our frailty. Our brokenness. Our inability. It's just as Paul tells us in 2 Corinthians 12:10: "When I am weak, then I am strong." We have to be willing to be human.

Maybe that means unpacking one of our stories, telling them what we were really like at their age. "Hey, I struggled in algebra too," we might say. "In fact . . ." We might even tell them how much we *still* hate algebra. Sure, we have to be careful to not turn these humanizing stories into ready-made excuses. We don't want our children to turn around and say, "Well, since Mom never got math, I guess that makes it OK to fail." But if we can tell them, through the lens of our own experience, how important something is (even if we didn't like to do it) or how there are some things in life we just need to get through (even if we'd rather not), we can make our children feel as though we're both in this together. This isn't "me versus you"; we're all on the same side. And when we follow this path, the blame game never gets started.

We have to guide our children. We're their caretakers, and sometimes that means correcting them when they make a mistake. Sometimes we need to correct our spouses and ourselves too.

Unhealthy blame is never the answer. There's always a better way.

When our children let us down, we can lift them up. When they make a mistake, we can tell them we've made mistakes too.

Ending the Game

This is your fault.

   I blame you.

   I'm better than you.

This is the language of blame. Words like this, even when they're unspoken but communicated nonverbally, can tear your family apart.

But words can heal too. Let me suggest a few.

It'll be OK.

I'm sorry.

I love you.

When we're hurt or angry, these are not easy words to say. Not when we want to lash out. Not when we're playing the game. To let go of our righteous anger feels like giving up Park Place and Boardwalk. That's no way to win, right?

But families aren't about winning; they're about growing. Teaching. Loving. We're here to give our kids the best possible foundation for thriving. And sometimes that means setting aside our own pride. Instead of using our finger to point out the wrong and who to blame, we use that finger to point to a better way, even to a solution.

On the cross, Jesus had all the reason in the world to blame. Everyone really was guilty: Pilate, Caiaphas, the Jews and the Romans, and all the sinners that made His sacrifice necessary. "This is *your* fault," He could have said to anyone who watched Him die. That blame would've been fully justified.

But Jesus didn't go there.

"Father, forgive them, for they do not know what they are doing," He said (Luke 23:34).

We all make mistakes. Our kids, still learning how to operate in this strange, broken world of ours, make mistakes too—and often way more mistakes than we'd like.

But we need to do more than just correct those mistakes when they happen. One of the most important lessons we can teach our children is how to forgive, like Christ forgave us. How to let go of blame. We need to teach them about grace and love, and the best way to teach them is to show them.

Chapter Eight

A SAFE PLACE

✦

I'd never been to a camp where a used Ziploc bag was a treasure.

"Camp Life" feels, in many ways, like a Christian camp you'd see anywhere in the United States. Kids come from all over the country for a week of fun and fellowship. They sing. They laugh at the funny skits. They clap and dance and play games. And then they break up for small group discussions, where their counselors—Jean, our boys, and I, among dozens of others—talk to them about God and faith.

But there was a big difference from an Awana camp back home and this summer camp in Lusaka, the capital of Zambia.

One afternoon after I'd eaten the peanut butter and jelly sandwich I'd made the night before (along with forty-seven more sandwiches), I stuffed the Ziploc bag into my pocket, just to get it out of the way. One of the kids saw it and pulled it out, and suddenly it was like a jailbreak. These cute, delightful children—boys who never failed to say "please" and "thank you," boys who called me "Uncle Jim," turned feral. They scrambled over the used bag like it was a Major League home run ball or a golden ring.

The sponsoring group, Family Legacy, warned me that these kids would fight over things we wouldn't believe, and they were right: I *didn't* believe it. Not until I saw it firsthand. For these children, my used Ziploc baggie, the same thing many of us mindlessly throw out almost every day, was a valuable commodity. It gave their families a place to store beans or rice.

Or it would have, had these boys had families.

Check out the United States population pyramid (a chart that illustrates a country's demographic breakdown from youngest to oldest, from bottom to top), and it looks like a steamship.[1] The population is relatively spread out among children and adults, with the ship bowing out slightly to account for the Baby Boomers before tapering up to the folks in their seventies and eighties. Look at Zambia's population pyramid, and it looks almost like a flagpole with a big base.[2] Children *far* outnumber adults in this country decimated by HIV/AIDS. The average life expectancy in Zambia is just fifty-seven years.

Most of the kids who come to Camp Life are double orphans. All are desperately poor. The Legacy Foundation finds the country's least of the least, kids sleeping on the streets, kids being abused by their aunts or uncles. They seemed genuinely happy at camp, smiling and laughing from breakfast to dinner. But each beaming face hid a lifetime of tragedy.

Moses, one of the boys in Trent's counseling group, had buried his mother just three days before camp. One of my kids got treated for ringworm every day. A girl in Jean's group, just twelve or thirteen years old, confessed that she'd been raped by her mother's boyfriend the first night her mom brought him home. He threatened to kill them both if she ever told.

"I wish camp would never end," these children would say in their Africanized accents. Kids say that in the United States too. But at Camp Life, there's a bleak poignancy to those words. A desperation. Once camp ends, some won't know where or when their next meal will come. Some fear what awaits them at home.

A safe place? Most of these children don't know what that is. And if they know a safe place, home isn't it.

And yet these kids are amazingly resilient and blessed with a remarkable capacity for compassion.

One morning during our small group discussion time, I told the ten boys I was counseling my *own* story. How my mother died when I was just a little boy. How my father died not long after. How I was pretty much on my own when I was a teen. You could see the kids' jaws drop—I was an orphan, just like them.

When I finished my story, one little boy reached over and patted me on the shoulder. He didn't say anything, but his meaning was clear. *It'll be OK*, he was telling me with his comforting, gentle pat. *It'll be OK.*

The rest of the week, the twelve-year-old boy clung to me. He held my hand all day long.

For a week, he found a semblance of safety at camp. Maybe he found a sense of comfort in me. And I wonder, looking back, whether he was trying to give me that same sense of safety and comfort—if he was telling me, like he was telling himself, *It'll be OK.*

A Refuge from the Storm

In the Daly family, if the boys start bickering—if one calls the other "stupid" or makes fun of him for something—Jean steps in.

"Hey!" she'll say. "Family's supposed to be a safe place! Family is a place where we *love* each other. Where we can be whoever we are. Be the *real* us."

I don't know if I've ever heard a better definition of what family is supposed to be. Jean's absolutely right. Family *should* equal safety. Ideally, it should be the safest place we'll ever know, the place we go back to when everything else in our lives blows up. Family is home. And home should be safe.

But families aren't always the safe places they should be. And the failures can be spectacular.

In Zambia, HIV/AIDS triggered both the suffering we observed firsthand and the country's overwhelming poverty. But I see these horrific societal ills as symptoms of a much more insidious disease— the breakdown of the family. Men are running away from their responsibilities, and when the family collapses, society struggles. People lose their sense of identity, their sense of basic decency. And who are the most vulnerable? The children. The boys who go to bed hungry. The girls who get ravaged by men who know no one will ever catch them. The children at this camp don't feel safe at home, even if they have one. For them, camp might be as close as they can get to feeling like a family should feel.

These kids know us for just a week. But before we leave, they're calling us "Uncle Jim," "Aunt Jean," "Uncle Trent," and "Uncle Troy." As soon as we get off the bus, they run to us and practically bowl us over. They jump into our arms. They cling to our legs. For just a few days, they feel safe. But for much of their lives—even around the people who are supposed to take care of them—they feel anything but safe.

And it's not as if such a lack of familial safety is an issue only "over there." It's here too—from Orange County to Iowa, from Manhattan to rural Missouri. Lack of safety inside the family isn't only a by-product of poverty. It all comes down to the sort of environment that parents willfully create for their kids, a sense of safety and belonging that's so critical to a child's well-being. And if parents don't create that environment, kids pay the price.

The government in Zambia is trying hard to make the changes needed to protect children. We talked to several social workers triaging the children according to the risks they face. The assignment feels overwhelming.

Abused children often have trouble regulating their own emotions. Experts say they're at a higher risk of developing a host of anxiety, personality, sexual, or eating disorders. Neglected kids often experience delays in their motor skills and social development. Children subjected to bullying (inside or outside the home) often see drops in their grades and have trouble sleeping. All of these kids can struggle with depression, anxiety, and a sense of hopelessness.

And the problems don't stop once children leave home. Kids from unsafe families often grow into anxious, troubled adults. When Tom and Beverly Rodgers visited the Focus on the Family daily broadcast, they described such troubles as *soul wounds*: "It impacts the sense of who we are and how we interact with our environment," Tom said. "And most of the time, because these wounds are developmental and occur very early in life, we simply internalize that wound—we're not lovable; something's wrong with us. And then we simply adapt to that message."

Family is supposed to be a safe place. But so often it's not.

I bet you have your own stories about how someone ripped away your own illusion of safety: When your mom came home drunk. When your dad left and never really came back. When someone hit you. When someone abused you. Many of us know what it's like to lose that harbor. Some of us have never even had one.

We know how important safety is in a family. We don't need to be told. But how do we create a family that feels safe? Stable? Secure?

First, we have to foster an environment where kids feel *physically safe*. This should be pretty obvious. No one should ever hit a child, no matter the circumstance. I'm not talking about spankings, a smack to the behind to reinforce an important message, but the thoughtless, out-of-control acts of violence that will instantly crush a child's sense of safety.

Comedian Jeff Allen frequently talks about the painful catalyst that changed his life—the moment he beat his infant son. (We used one of his talks on the Focus on the Family broadcast.) He was drunk, he says. His little boy was crying. He lashed out, and the boy's mother pulled him away and carried him down the hall—the boy sobbing, head on his mother's shoulder.

"And as I walked toward him, I got under the light in the hall, and my son, six months old, got a look at me and his eyes filled with fear," Allen recalled. "And I realized that I put that fear in that innocent child's life. And he sat on the bed with my wife, and my wife fed him. He got beat because he was hungry."

Three days later, Jeff began going to Alcoholics Anonymous. It became the catalyst to turn around his life, repair a flailing marriage, and find Christ.

But parents don't need to leave a bruise to rob a child of that sense of safety.

Flailing

My dad never hit me. He never even spanked me. When he got drunk, he'd threaten my mom, and my older brother, Mike, would jump between them. Mike took a lot of blows from my dad, and like so many others, he still lives with the scars of that abuse. As the baby of the family, I was always protected by someone. But while I was off-limits from that sort of abuse, my dad could hurt me in other ways.

One afternoon when I was very young, the whole family went to the pool. As I sat at the edge, dangling my feet in the water, my dad just up and threw me into the deep end.

"It's time to learn how to swim!" he said as the water covered me, pouring into my startled lungs and stomach as I sank in nine feet of water. Mike pulled me out.

I learned that afternoon that I couldn't trust my dad. I couldn't count on him to be that harbor for me. From then on, I was on my guard around him, always worried about what he might do. Home, family, was never truly safe for me again.

It's just as important to create a home where kids feel *emotionally safe*. Where they're not on edge, where (as Jean reminds our boys) they can be themselves and still be loved.

We can foster this environment through strong, reasonable boundaries, both for parents and children. All of us, whether we know it or not, find comfort in structure. We find comfort in the knowable, the predictable. And the more stressful life is outside the family, the more our children will crave structure and predictability inside it. According to the experts, children who've gone through a traumatic event desperately need structure *somewhere*. That structure allows them to recover and gives them the time and space to find their footing again.

Think of the family—that safe, comfortable "home" we want to create for our kids—as a literal house. We can't just build one in a day out of drywall and paint without a few two-by-sixes underneath. We need a solid, strong framework in place. We need a structure that defines what our home will look like and how it'll operate. That structure supports our floor and roof and walls. It keeps us dry in the rain and warm in the snow. If that structure is strong enough and the planning behind it thorough enough, it can even protect us from disaster.

So it is with the family. The structure of a family—the boundaries we place on ourselves—is critical to creating a healthy home.

So as parents, we must first place some healthy boundaries on *ourselves*, even before we start creating them for our children. Why? It goes back to structure and predictability. Our kids need to know what to expect from us. They don't need dads who push them unexpectedly into the pool. They don't need moms who might come home drunk and out of control. They don't need parents who react to problems in anger or frustration. If we expect our children to obey our rules, we need to submit to some rules ourselves. Once we do that, we can move on to rules for our children.

Children naturally need boundaries—predictable, reliable limitations that don't shift by the hour. Now, I doubt you need a lot of rules in a well-functioning family. In fact, lots of experts say the fewer rules you have, the better. But whatever rules and expectations you have, they need to be clearly defined and steadily, reasonably enforced.

That's where things get especially tricky.

It's so easy to read the paragraph above and slip into a rigid, legalistic mind-set as a parent. Sure, it's important for kids to understand where their boundaries are. Yes, it's important that we correct our kids when they cross those boundaries or break our rules. But we can't lose sight of the importance of grace and the critical element of forgiveness. We have to learn the delicate balance between leading and teaching and being sure not to crush our children's spirits.

Soft Boundaries

As parents, we naturally reinforce the behavior we want to see. We want our kids to work hard, treat people with respect, obey us when we tell them to mow the lawn. But as we try to reinforce these behaviors, we can do so with a demeaning, belittling, or even cruel attitude. And sometimes, even when we correct them with the best of intentions, what we say (or what we *mean* to say) and what they hear can be very different.

We may tell our children, "You're not being diligent enough. You're not disciplined enough. You're not polite enough." *You're not, you're not, you're not.* Children have a hard time hearing a lot of "you're nots." Eventually it communicates to them, *You're not good enough.* Perhaps you tell your child she's not doing her homework—a clear fact. But you may enlarge that statement with a host of other "you're nots," or if you keep pounding this one note all the time, eventually you'll stop communicating the lesson you intended. At best, the child may just zone out: *Oh, Mom's on another one of her warpaths again.* At worst, you're communicating that the child just isn't measuring up. You're communicating that she's just not worthy. And that's not a safe place to be.

I sometimes see that dynamic at work in my own kids. We expect our boys to keep up their grades, tend to their personal hygiene, follow the Golden Rule—all good, important things, but things that boys (and girls too) sometimes struggle to master as children of thirteen or fourteen. All those factors can lead to an avalanche of "you're not" speeches. And when it gets pervasive—for example, when Jean or I

corrected, instructed, or blamed Trent every time he came within
earshot—it wore on him. You could see it pulling him down, lecture
by lecture.

Let's return to the house metaphor. We have our framework, the
underlying structure of the home. It holds everything in place. But
as fundamental as that underlying structure is, a home that consisted
of nothing *but* that framework would be a very poor home indeed.
Sure, it might stand for a hundred years, but you wouldn't want to
live there for even a day. In most homes, that framework is *hidden*.
We all know it's there, but it's covered with drywall and paint, carpet,
and popcorn ceilings. It's festooned with art, dappled by windows. It
supports couches perfect for afternoon naps, and dining room tables
where we might spend hours playing Payday or Risk.

The same principles apply as we try to build safe families. Sure,
the framework is important, and the structure critical. But we don't
need to see it all the time. Most days, we should barely know it's there.
We cover it with laughter and affection. We coat it with our memories.
We decorate it with our love and grace.

When I think about how this reality manifests in a family, I
return again and again to the example set by my friend Danie van
den Heever, a South African businessman. When I'm in his country
and at his house for dinner and his children get out of line (and they
do), he doesn't correct them with a scowl and a reprimand. He turns
it into an opportunity to shower even more love on the child.

"Rudy, Rudy, Rudy," he'll say with a smile, pulling Rudy over to
him gently, affectionately wrapping him in a hug. "Let's talk." There's
no hint of a "you're not" rebuke in there: *You're not supposed to do that.*
You're not living up to my expectations. You're not . . . anything. It's the
opposite: *You are. You are my son. You are loved. You are so special to*
me, and because of that, I want you to do better.

How do you build a family that feels safe? You need structure. You
need grace. Both critical components work together. But be aware:
some kids need more of one thing and less of the other.

Rules and Grace

As mentioned earlier, we're hosting a couple of foster kids right now. But not everyone in our family wanted to do it.

Several years ago, we decided to help a couple of *other* foster children, nine-year-old Joe and eight-year-old Jack (again, not their real names). We hoped to be a positive influence in these boys' lives. We figured they could use a little stability. They needed to feel safe. We thought it'd be great if we could give that to them.

But we didn't imagine how deeply our own kids might be affected, and what a difficult experience it would be for Troy.

Of our two boys, Troy thrives the most in structure. He's our straight-A student, the guy who's always ready to talk about God and spirituality, the son who seems to succeed in almost everything set before him. He excels in an environment where he knows the rules, because he'll always be willing and able and even excited to follow them. And for him, our home life was pretty idyllic. The well-defined structure of our home suited him to a tee. He exuded joy.

But when Joe and Jack arrived, they upset the structure. Even as we Dalys tried to give them some much-needed stability, they wound up destabilizing our home. They were raised in a much different environment, with a much different structure than the one Troy was used to. They cursed and fought. And when they weren't fighting with each other, they'd sometimes turn on Troy. They bullied Troy in his own home. And suddenly this safe place of his, his family refuge, didn't feel so safe anymore.

When we were given a new foster opportunity in 2016, we got pulled into the conversation pretty late in the game. These kids needed a new home immediately. We had to make a decision quickly. So we gathered for a brief family meeting to discuss whether we wanted to bring Jerilee and John into our home.

"I don't want to do it," Troy told us flatly. "I know you guys all want to do it, and so we're going to do it, but I don't want to. That's where I'm at." He'd had a bad experience once. His structure had been upended the last time. His security had been blown. He didn't want it to happen again.

What a contrast to Trent's reaction. "C'mon, Troy," he said. "We gotta help these kids. They're in a bad spot. It's the right thing to do."

Trent, my struggling student, the one I'm always getting on, the one whom Jean and I worry about the most, showed this beautiful heart. *C'mon, Troy. It's the right thing to do.* It caught me. *I see his heart, Lord,* I remember thinking. *I see his heart.*

Well, Troy was right about one thing: We welcomed in a new set of foster kids against his objections. And even though these young children can't bully anyone, Troy still struggles with it—nothing like the previous situation, but he's still not comfortable. The structure that he thrives in has been upended once more. Frankly, I'm a little more like Troy in this regard.

Both of us can learn something from Trent.

Trent's all-in with these kids. If they ask him to play with them, boom, he's there. If they need help doing something, he's right beside them. Whatever the kids need, he's willing to help.

The attitude is wildly different from what we've seen in some other areas of his life. If I ask him to do homework, I get pushback. "Why? Why do I have to do it now?" But if John asks him to play a game, he's there. "Of course," he'll say. "No problem." When it comes to our foster children, Trent shows an amazing attitude and heart.

It makes me wonder why.

I think it comes down to the concept of safety. If Troy thrives in structure, Trent sometimes rebels against it. The boundaries—and Jean's and my frequent lectures for him to heed those boundaries—can drive him a little crazy. In fact, I wonder if all those lectures can make him feel unsafe. They stress him out. Sometimes it can seem that our conversations are always about school and performance. Maybe with these foster children, Trent is showing us more of the attitude he wants—maybe needs—to see in our home. Kindness. Understanding. Grace.

If Troy is all about the framing and the rafters, Trent is all about the comfy couch. And even if his mother and I sometimes have to drag him off the couch to do his homework, maybe Trent's own understanding of what a safe family looks like makes him more able to give security to others.

Flying

In Africa, Trent was in his element. The kids at Camp Life connected with us all, but they seemed to have a special affinity for Trent. Part of it is just his size. He's six foot four, so he's like a huge tree they can climb on. They feel that physical stability in him. That *structure*, if you will.

But it's more than that. He has an inner strength too, a calming demeanor. Nothing rattled him in Zambia; its unfamiliarity didn't fluster him. I think the kids could feel a quiet strength inside him, something that went deeper than his frame and build. They could feel *safe* with him. It amazed me. And because they felt safe, they could feel happy, exuberant, and even joyful.

A paradox lies at the heart of every safe family: Safe kids are brave kids. Adventurous kids. Daring kids. Children who don't feel safe at home tend to be cautious and fearful, scared of not measuring up. Children who *do* feel safe—well, they don't fear making messes. Taking chances doesn't frighten them. If kids know their family has their backs, they can face forward—face their futures—with confidence.

With my boys now in their teens, I see that so plainly. I want them to feel safe enough at home, safe enough with me, to tell me anything. If they're in trouble, if they've made a mistake, I want to know about it. I want to be able to help. But there's no way that'll happen if our family isn't a safe place to share and to be ourselves. The necessary level of comfort just won't exist. They'll feel afraid.

I want my boys to feel like they can say anything to me, even if they know it'll hurt or disappoint me. I want them to feel a little like those children in Zambia felt around Trent. I want them to feel that stability, that inner strength. I want them to feel as safe around me when they're eighteen as they felt when I could pick them up in my hands and hold them in the air.

Because when you trust the hands that hold you, you gain the ability to soar.

Chapter Nine

ACCEPTING FREE WILL

✦

Andrew excelled at everything he wanted to do. And he wanted to rebel.

As a world-class mischief maker, he and his friend Bailey would drop a jug of gasoline onto an open road and set it ablaze, "just for kicks." They'd turn rubber-cement jars into makeshift Molotov cocktails, replacing the bristles with wicks, lighting them, and throwing them against the school wall, watching the flames spread over the goo.

His parents tried to rein Andrew in, and at times it seemed to work. He could play the good kid when he needed to. But he never repented. And as Andrew changed from boy to teen, he slowly moved from trying to set other things on fire to setting his own life ablaze.

"From the youngest of ages, me and my friends would sneak outta the house and rip off our neighbors' liquor cabinets," he said during a speech that was later broadcast on Focus on the Family. "We could get a bag of dope anywhere."

He and his pals would smuggle marijuana and liquor bottles onto the ski lift during youth group ski trips. At high school keggers, he'd drink himself to near oblivion and sometimes drive home. And once he went to college, away from the supervision of his caring Christian parents, things got even worse. By the time Andrew was twenty, he was almost completely out of control. Disinterested in God, he lived for the next drink and the next party.

Through it all, Andrew's parents struggled to preserve their relationship with their wayward son. Even when they couldn't keep their eyes on him physically or control him emotionally, they remained a presence in his life.

In 1987, just as Andrew was turning twenty-one, they were due to take a family vacation in Whistler, Canada, the trip of a lifetime. A friend had loaned them the use of his house over Andrew's spring break, and Mom and Dad saved and scrounged every penny to make the trip possible for their family of five.

But Andrew had joined a frat at the University of Oregon, and his "brothers" weren't about to let him leave without throwing him a twenty-first birthday party for the ages.

Four days later, the tequila still flowed and the party still rolled on, at least for Andrew. By the time Andrew's mom finally called the frat house phone and talked with him, a drunken Andrew was two days late to his own family vacation.

Did I mention Andrew's last name? It's Palau. He's the son of Pat and Luis Palau, the legendary evangelist.

Different Paths

Life is a journey. We've all heard the clichés. People talk about these metaphorical roads on our journey all the time: the road to success, the road to financial freedom, the road to salvation. Bob Dylan asks us how many roads we have to walk down before we grow up. Yogi Berra tells us, "When you come to a fork in the road, take it."

The Bible is full of journey-of-life metaphors: "In all your ways submit to him, and he will make your paths straight," we're told in Proverbs 3:6. A chapter later, in Proverbs 4:27, we read, "Do not turn to the right or the left; keep your foot from evil."

But so often, we still ignore the Bible's wisdom and blaze our own trail now and then. Some of us skip alongside the path for a time, getting caught in the brambles but never truly losing sight of where we're headed. Others barrel headlong into the forest, crashing through thickets like drunken deer, tumbling down hills and splashing through rivers. "Forget the path," they say. "I'll make my own."

The parable of the prodigal son may be one of the most famous stories in all of Scripture. In the story told by Jesus (recorded in Luke 15), we learn that a father had two sons. One of the sons asks his father, prematurely, for his share of the family estate and then bolts to a foreign country, where he "squandered his wealth in wild living" (verse 13). He forged his own path, and it carried him straight out of Dodge. If the story happened today, we'd imagine the prodigal behind the wheel of a muscle car with fuzzy dice hanging from the rearview mirror, a bottle of cheap scotch in the passenger seat, a couple of joints in his pocket, and his GPS giving him directions straight to Vegas.

Many moms and dads see the story of the prodigal son as painfully familiar. Maybe their kids aren't outright squandering the family fortune, but it can feel like they're frittering away their birthright and wasting their lives. The worry begins early—the first time one of them punches another kid in kindergarten or cheats on a quiz in second grade. Did your daughter get a D in history? Time to worry. Son caught smoking in the bathroom? Set aside extra prayer time for that boy. Did she cut class? Did he look at some dirty pictures on the Internet? You start looking into the legality of installing tracking chips in your kids and security cameras in your house.

Often that worry is warranted. Andrew Palau is proof of that. But sometimes we parents think our kids are running headlong into oblivion when in reality they just took a step or two off the path. And sometimes we worry even when they haven't actually strayed from their *own* path at all.

It all goes back to our preoccupation with perfection. We want our kids to do well. We want them to excel. That's only natural, even if it can lead at times to unhealthy pressure and expectations. But a lot of times we take it a step further. We not only want them to excel;

we want them to excel in the very same things *we* excelled in, or focus on the things *we* place a priority on or the things *we* feel should be important to *them*. We want their paths to look like ours (or how ours would've looked had we avoided our own share of straying). Often, that's just not the way God plots it out.

We *think* we know what our kids' paths should look like. But do we really? Should we really feel concerned that our children have taken the path to Andrew Palau–size prodigalism if they go to a risqué website?

Some parents dub their children prodigals-in-the-making, not because they're bad, but because they're just not as good as their parents want them to be. They're *not good enough*. And sometimes, with enough angst and pressure from Mom and Dad, that prodigal label becomes a prophecy. The more you tell children how wayward they are, the more likely it is that they'll fulfill those expectations.

In 2014, I talked with Dr. Kathy Koch and Jill Savage about their book *No More Perfect Kids*. Kathy told me about how some of the children she counsels tear themselves apart trying to please their parents. But no matter how hard they try, they fail. They simply lack the tools to do what their moms and dads expect them to do.

She uses the example of a father talking to his child about a math grade. "Your grade needs to be higher," Dad says. So she works harder, studies longer, and gets help from the teacher after class. And guess what? It pays off. The child raises her grade to a 93. But that improvement doesn't satisfy the father. For him, that 93 percent is still 7 percent lower than it should be. It speaks to a work ethic that could be improved, a young mind that should be more disciplined. *Not good enough.*

"I have tears in my eyes, because the dads—they don't have any intentionality of hurting their children," Kathy told me. "They deeply desire the best for them, and they believe a 100 percent is best. *Is* it best? If the child is capable of the 100 percent, of course it is. But for a lot of children, the 93 *is* their 100 percent."

Their best still falls short of their father's expectations. And eventually, the child will ask herself, *Why even try? If my best is going to still disappoint, what's the point in doing my best?*

Our children will fail. That's a fact. But all too often, parents see those moments of failure as signs of *failed children*. The kids have gone wrong somewhere. The parents have failed too. Kathy reminds us that it's critical for parents to keep a sense of perspective during those inevitable stumbles, the messes along the way. "Did they make a mistake intentionally, to push a button, to get a reaction?" she asks. "Are they giving up because they're choosing to be apathetic? Or were they really making an honest attempt to earn an A in biology or to do well in the piano recital—and something just happened; they just didn't do their best? Well, good heavens! I don't always do *my* best. I'm very grateful for people who surround *me* with love in those moments."

We need to remember that. None of us *always* do our best. We don't always follow the lessons we're trying to teach our children. We fail too. We make foolish mistakes. We stray from the path. Does that make *us* prodigals? Do *we* become rebellious failures when we squander, even momentarily, the gifts our heavenly Father gave to us?

The only real difference between our failures and our children's is that our report cards don't get emailed home.

We all have different paths. Our paths are not our children's paths. That simple truth can make parenthood really frustrating. And it gets particularly frustrating when *we think we know* our children are leaving the path set out before them.

Making the Grade?

It amazes me how technology has given us parents the ability to track every step of our children's education. Back when I was growing up, the school just sent home a quarterly report card. That was it. But now, thanks to the Internet and smart phones, parents can go online and instantly check out test scores, homework assignments, current grade statuses—pretty much anything.

Bad news for Trent.

Shortly before a speaking engagement a couple of years ago, I happened to go online to check on Trent's history grade. And what did I find? Last homework assignment: missing. The one before that: missing. Syllabus: missing. Mesopotamia report: missing. Out of fifty possible points, Trent had missed all fifty.

BOOM.

Since I'm always eager to reinforce to my audiences that no family's perfect, including mine, I approached the podium, held up my phone, and said, "Hey, let me show you what I just read about three minutes ago!"

Now, I don't think a bad grade in history is reason to set off the prodigal alarm, necessarily. Jean gets more worried than I do about the scope of these signs. But my son's lack of effort concerned me too. This wasn't a case of Trent working his hardest and just not reaching our expectations; this was Trent not working *at all*. As parents, we always try to gauge how our children are doing, how well they're staying on the path, from a limited number of signs. Grades and schoolwork aren't the be-all and end-all, but they are among the few indicators we have of who they're growing into and who they're going to be. It's easy as a parent to look at that indicator and worry. As parents, we see a D or an F, and we imagine that our darling son or daughter is on the road to becoming an ax murderer.

And so in the Daly house, we pushed Trent for better grades. More importantly, we pushed for better effort.

Honestly, we're still pushing.

On *My Three Sons*, one of my favorite TV programs growing up, problems got solved in thirty minutes sharp. In parenting books, they can get tidily wrapped up in a chapter or two. Real life, unfortunately, doesn't work that way. We rarely solve big issues in one family meeting or one heart-to-heart talk. More often, they simmer for months or even years. Every day, it seems, we wake up and try to solve the same problems in different ways. Sometimes we bribe; other times we threaten. We may try a friendly joke as motivation one week and then jump to outright screaming the next. We trot out bribes and punishments in equal measure, and still, nothing seems to work.

The Daly family is no different. For years, the three of us—Jean, Trent, and I—have grappled with Trent's occasional struggles in school. We all know he's plenty smart. And Jean especially wants to see him put more of an emphasis on his schoolwork, particularly homework. She wants to see his work habits kicked into a higher gear. She wants him to *get it*. She wants him to understand the value of school, both as an intrinsic joy (she loved school) and a pragmatic necessity (to get into a good college). And she's done everything she can to make Trent *get it*. And she keeps trying. Because she hopes maybe there's a secret button somewhere or some lever she might pull with just the right combination of words and circumstances. If she could physically *make* Trent get his homework done, force his hand to paper and scratch out the work, line by line, I think she would.

But I doubt very much that Trent doesn't get it. He's a teenager, and he doesn't *want* to do homework. And the more we push, the more we try to make it happen, the less he wants to do it.

Jean turns to me for support in these ongoing struggles. She says, "Do something." And so I try. I lecture and scold and encourage.

But we can't really *make* our son do anything. That window of command and control ends at about ten years of age.

Own It

Newborns are helpless little things. They depend on you for food and shelter and fresh diapers. You have almost limitless control over them. They never question your authority. And even as they begin to explore their independence—the so-called "terrible twos" that can often last a lot longer—there's still no question who's in charge. If they absolutely refuse to leave the grocery store, you can simply pick them up and carry them out. Even as they grow into preschool, a child's world revolves around Mom and Dad.

But then things begin to change. The child realizes that Mom might not automatically know if he steals a cookie from the cookie jar before dinner. He starts to figure out, *Hey, I have a little control here.* In that child's eyes, we parents go from godlike beings to household bosses—still in charge, but not omniscient and certainly not infallible. Before long, kids stop accepting rules simply "because I said so." By the time the child becomes a teen, moms and dads can look very fallible indeed. (Ironically, even as we keep pushing for our children to be perfect, our kids know, by the time they're fourteen, how imperfect *we* are.)

I think most parents instinctively understand that you can't parent a twelve-year-old girl the same way you would a two-year-old. As our children grow, our parenting strategies change. We physically stuff those creamed carrots into our infants' mouths. As they get older and make faces at the sight of orange vegetables, we give them an age-appropriate choice: eat your carrots and you'll get dessert, or stay at the dinner table all night until you down them—a carrot-or-the-stick approach, if you will. Years later, if they *still* don't want to eat their veggies, we try to reason with them. We tell them how important vegetables are to a balanced diet, how many vitamins they have, how starving children in Africa would *love* to have a dish of cooked, glazed carrots. We understand that *forcing* our children to eat those carrots—and, by extension, forcing them to make the right decisions—won't always work. The whole point of parenting is to train your children to make good decisions on their own, not because you say so, but because they want to. Because they know it's the right thing to do.

We begin to aim our lessons not simply at that one healthy decision, but to boost our child's overall character. We show him or her that the decisions they make now say something about who they are and what they value. We show them that the decisions they make today will impact their lives tomorrow. We teach them how to make wise choices because we won't always be around to help them.

But even though we see this as the end goal of our jobs as moms and dads—to give our children tools to make good decisions on their own—we refuse to allow them to learn from their bad decisions. We sometimes forbid those bad choices even from being made. Even when our children reach their teen years, a part of us still wants to shove the right choice down their throats.

As if we could.

Trent stands six foot four. I can't *make* him do anything. He's a strong-willed kid, which means he won't do something just because Mom and Dad tell him to. He's never accepted the "because I said so" line. Even as a little guy, Trent has needed to know the *why* and the *how come*. And like most teens, he's trying to figure out what kind of person he wants to be. He's pushing boundaries. He's defining himself. He's figuring out what it looks like to be an adult.

Jean and I can talk with him about homework until all three of us are sick of it. We can reason with him and tell him about the importance of studying, how his future depends on good grades *now*. We can force him to sit at the dining room table with his history or algebra book open, hoping he'll study it or, if that's too much to hope for, that some knowledge will just leap off the page and somehow stick in his head. But we can't *make* him succeed. We can't *make* him share our educational values. At this point in Trent's life, the decision is ultimately his to make, and the consequences are his too.

I don't know what to do other than to let him own it. He must own it. I don't have the power or skill set to *make* him do anything.

Oh, and by the way, it seems God rejected that skill set too. Yeah, think about *that* for a minute.

In *The Great Divorce*, C. S. Lewis wrote, "There are only two kinds of people in the end: those who say to God, 'Thy will be done,' and those to whom God says, in the end, '*Thy* will be done.' All that are in Hell, choose it."[1]

God could've made us much different creatures. He could've made us in such a way that we'd all invariably make the right decisions. He could've made sure we spent our lives worshiping and honoring Him. He could've *made* us be good people and forced those spiritual carrots down our throats for all eternity.

But God didn't do that. He gave us free will. He gave us the ability to make our own choices, even bad ones.

I believe this truth forces us parents to ask ourselves, *Is it really part of the equation to command and control our son's or daughter's decisions? Is God really expecting us to force them to make the right choices?* I doubt it. Definitely not in the case of teenagers.

So then, we have to ask ourselves another question: Why?

The Importance of Failure

When one of our boys was having a little trouble in seventh grade, Jean and I went to talk with the principal, hoping he'd have some advice for us. I'll never forget what he said.

"If they're going to fail, let them fail now," he told us. "Better to fail in seventh grade than in twelfth. Better to learn a hard, painful lesson about prioritization and coping skills now than in their freshman year of college."

Parents don't want their children to fail in anything. I get that. We don't like messes, and failure is messy. We tell our children to learn from their mistakes, but we rarely let them make any.

And let's face it, a good chunk of our parenting makeup, our mom and dad genes, is geared to protecting our children from failure. We don't want them to feel pain or to suffer setbacks. From the beginning of their lives as helpless babies wrapped in our arms, we've done everything we can do to protect them. We put safety corners on our coffee tables, plop bicycle helmets on their heads, and tell them to never, ever talk with strangers. We do everything in our power to keep our kids safe. I just spent a full chapter stressing the importance of creating a safe environment for our sons and daughters. We *need* safe families, safe homes.

But as much as we foster safe places inside our families, the world outside is dangerous. And it always will be.

We live a life filled with pain. Angst. Stress. Setbacks. Failure. How nice if our children could avoid it all—just bypass the pain and failure with some wise, good decisions. But they won't make all wise and good decisions. So if our children are going to fail, better to let them fail now. Better to let them break a little when you're there to help pick up the pieces.

Failure seems to be a part of God's plan. In fact, when we read the Bible, it sometimes seems as if failure helps us grow emotionally and spiritually more than our successes.

That doesn't mean our failures won't hurt! They will, and maybe that's part of the point. When Jacob wrestled with God in the desert, his hip popped out of joint (Genesis 32:25). Jacob walked with a limp after that, perhaps for the rest of his days. But after that he walked closer to God too.

Our children will struggle. They will fail. And sometimes our children may run away from everything we tried to teach them. But by God's grace, they'll come home again. Hurt, sure. Limping, perhaps. But coming home.

Let's make sure we keep the door unlocked for them.

The Prodigal

You might've thought that after Andrew Palau's four-day bender nearly ruined the family vacation to Whistler, he would've straightened up. But he didn't. Not really. He considered that shameful moment simply a blip on his party train. While his partying habits slowed a bit after graduation, they did so only because he knew he needed to work the next morning. And just because he didn't stay out all night like he used to didn't mean he never went to bed drunk.

Andrew's parents knew he wasn't in a good spot. They talked with him about his decisions. They prayed tirelessly. And because Andrew had drifted away from God, they encouraged him to come back to his faith.

Most importantly, they continued to love their wayward son. Even when Andrew rejected everything they stood for, Luis and Pat never stopped being a presence, an influence, however tiny, in his life.

"They did everything they could," he said. "But in the end, they just recognized that if anything good was going to happen in my life, it was going to be God's work. When God says He offers life—and life in abundance—He means it."

But God takes His time.

Andrew was twenty-seven when his father and mother invited him to Jamaica to attend one of Luis's crusades. Andrew said he'd attend as long as he could go fishing for marlin too. His dad said he could and even arranged a fishing trip. Andrew expected the trip to be merely another great opportunity for some fun and sun. He envisioned drinking beer on the beach, not undergoing a change of heart or finding a new direction in life. After all, he wasn't like the sheep his father preached to year after year. He'd heard it all a thousand times. Maybe literally.

But something happened this time, his thousandth-and-first. Andrew met some amazing people doing some amazing things through God's power. He began looking at his own life in a new way. And as he sat in Kingston National Stadium, the heat and humidity covering him like a blanket, he knew something else was pressing down on him—the Lord Himself.

"And I just knew," Andrew said, choking up, "this is not my parents. This is God Himself calling to me. And in this one moment, I'll never forget it, I kind of turned my phrasing from challenging God to reveal Himself to me to instead just asking Him to do one more thing for me. I just called out to Him in desperation. I said, 'God, what is keeping me from You?'

"And it's as if He just said, 'Aha. Do you really want to know, Andrew, what's keeping Me from you?' And I was like, 'Yes, what is it?' And He just opened up my eyes to see in that moment what was keeping me from Him—just all of that garbage in my life. I knew in that moment I was just broken. And I was bawling and bawling my head off."

Andrew's life turned around that day.

Andrew owned his life, his decisions. His parents couldn't change him. Only he and God could do that. But they did keep the door open. They never stopped loving him. They never gave up on him. They never stopped calling him "son."

The Importance of Patience

What's the most important tool in a parent's toolbox when a child goes prodigal? What's the most important thing we can do when our children, whether thirteen or thirty-three, shuck our advice and go their own way? We can wait. We can show patience.

All of the fundamentals remain critically important in these difficult seasons—the laughter, the listening, the Golden Rule. In fact, that Rule, that deceptively simple directive to "do to others what you would have them do to you," is something that we parents have to lean into ourselves more than ever. How would we want to be treated if we went off the rails? I think we'd want to be treated with love, understanding, and patience.

We parents can find this very hard. We want to give our kids what we think they need, a good kick in the rear, mostly, instead of what they want. And *of course* there's a critical place for honest, difficult conversations and corrective action. But remember, we're talking about our daughters and sons who have seemingly stopped listening to us.

Our words no longer sway them, nor do our bribes, punishments, or threats. They're determined to go their own way. And we must finally say to them, "*Thy* will be done."

Patience doesn't come easily, especially in an era of instant gratification. Not in an age of perfection-based parenting. We want things *right*, and we want them *right now*. To be patient seems to be passivity in the face of failure. It feels like giving up. We, to the contrary, want to fix things, clean things. It feels uncomfortably unnatural to let someone we love sit in the middle of their own mess and not at least *try* to make things right again.

Maybe that's why the Bible spends so much time reminding us to wait. "The LORD is good to those who wait for him . . . It is good that one should wait quietly for the salvation of the LORD," Lamentations 3:25–26 (ESV) reads. "And now, O Lord, for what do I wait? My hope is in you," we read in Psalm 39:7 (ESV). "For the revelation awaits an appointed time," Habakkuk 2:3 reads. "It speaks of the end and will not prove false. Though it linger, wait for it; it will certainly come and will not delay."

God knows we're not a patient people. He knows our need for resolution. He knows the anguish we feel when one of our children seems to go astray, the helplessness we feel when we can do nothing about it. And yet He asks us to wait.

And then maybe, after what may seem like a million years, the waiting pays off.

According to LifeWay Research, 70 percent of young adults drop out of church, usually during college.[2] But the same study found that two-thirds of those young adults eventually return. They leave the ways of their (often authoritarian) parents and make their own way for a while, sleeping around, smoking pot, rejecting apparently everything their parents taught them. But then something clicks. They get married. They have children themselves. They take on a mortgage. Suddenly, their "out of touch" parents don't look so out of touch anymore. Maybe they even look a little wise.

It took a famine for the prodigal son in Jesus' parable to come home. It took Andrew Palau a literal come-to-Jesus moment in Jamaica. But for many others, it just takes time—time to mature, to understand. Jill Savage talked on our broadcast about one of her own daughters, a prodigal throughout her teen years. Now an adult, that same daughter sometimes parrots the lessons Jill taught her. When Jill asked her about it, she simply said, "I was listening, Mom."

That's what we have to remember. Even when it seems they've closed their ears, our children are listening to us. Our lessons continue to seep into their resistant selves bit by bit, even when they're rebelling.

Studies show that even when our kids become teens and actively push away from us, we remain the number one influence in their lives. We continue to influence them, more than their teachers, more than their peers, more than any of the music or television shows or social networking blasts they see. They may not admit it, but they care about what we say and think. They're listening.

Dr. Kevin Leman is one of the country's most respected child-rearing experts and a guest on the Focus on the Family broadcast countless times. But to hear him tell it, he was a terror as a teen.

He brought home one report card in ninth grade in which he was failing every single subject. He earned an algebra grade of a whopping 22 percent. And while his grades improved as high school went on, it wasn't by much. He graduated fourth from the bottom of his class.

"My guidance counselor told me he couldn't get me in reform school," he told Jean and me on the broadcast in 2015. "My wife's head nurse said, 'Don't associate with that janitor. He'll never amount to anything.' And yet, I had a mom and dad—a mom who prayed for me every day of my life—a mom and dad who believed in me every day of my life. And they had very little reason to believe. But they prayed; they covered me with prayer every day."

In his early twenties, Kevin began to mature. He began to put the pieces together. On another broadcast, he talked about driving back to his old high school, where he was to be honored on the school's Wall of Fame. His ninety-five-year-old mother, the same woman who saw his 22 percent algebra grade all those years ago, accompanied him.

"Ma, we fooled a few people, didn't we?" Kevin told her. And his mother answered with all the pride you'd expect.

"Oh, honey," she said, "I am so proud of you. A mother couldn't be more proud of a son."

That pride was a long time in coming, but it came. And since I've interviewed Kevin so many times, I can't help but see some similarities between him and Trent. And I start to think, *OK, do I have a Kevin Leman here?*

The Other Prodigal

Kevin Leman has some simple advice for parents: "Failure is important. Grace, why is grace so abundant? Could it be that we need it? Could it be that our kids need it?"

But let's follow up with another question, one we don't think about very often. If failure is so important, where does that leave the kids who *don't* fail? If grace is so important, where does that leave the kids who very rarely need it?

Ironically, this is where I worry about Troy.

The kid is so *good*. He has great grades and strong character. He rarely gives his mother or me grief. I'm so proud of him in so many ways. He's as solid as I can imagine—dare I say "near perfect"? Naturally, we heap the praise on him. "Oh, I'm so proud of you. You're doing so well. Thanks for being such a great kid." I know he gets sick of it.

And so we reinforce how much we value his behavior. We praise him for his dutifulness, leadership, and example.

I wonder whether Jean and I are training Troy to seek *perfection*, even as I'm telling you that the quest for it is a bad, unhealthy thing. And I wonder: Are we teaching him to overvalue that praise? To overvalue behavioral habits above the true character of the soul? What happens when he leaves home and goes to college, where we're not around to praise him anymore? When he's away from that constant parental reinforcement, could he spin out of control? Become an Andrew Palau–like party animal? Could *he* become the prodigal?

And I have another, even odder worry. What if he stays on that straight, parental-approved, life-giving path for all the rest of his days? Does that bring its own share of danger?

When we read about the prodigal son in the Bible, we often see just one prodigal in the story. But actually there are two.

Jesus could have ended the story at Luke 15:24, with the prodigal returning and the father rejoicing. "Quick! Bring the best robe and put it on him. Put a ring on his finger and sandals on his feet," the father says (verse 22). "For this son of mine was dead and is alive again; he was lost and is found" (verse 24). What a beautiful ending! A happy ending, brimming with love and grace and forgiveness.

But Jesus doesn't end the story there. He draws our attention to the older son, the son who stayed dutifully on the ranch, who never got out of line, who did exactly what his dad wanted him to do. He sees the party his father throws for his wayward younger brother, and he gets angry: "Look! All these years I've been slaving for you and never disobeyed your orders. Yet you never gave me even a young goat so I could celebrate with my friends. But when this—" and you can almost hear him spit the next words—"son of yours who has squandered your property with prostitutes comes home, you kill the fattened calf for him!" (verses 29–30).

It doesn't seem fair. It doesn't seem right.

Parents aren't the only ones who get caught up in the quest for perfection. Sometimes children do too.

Although no one's perfect, some of us seem pretty good by society's standards. We've done our best all through life. Maybe we need to be forgiven for a little stolen cookie here or there, but that's it. Such a record can make it very difficult for those pretty good people to sympathize with folks—children, siblings—who mess up all the time. In this parable, it seems as if God asks us to shower our grace on people with almost unseemly abundance, and to spend that grace like the prodigal spent his fortune. God doesn't seem to care if it's right or just or even deserved. Grace, Jesus seems to tell us, is meant to be given in oversized portions.

But that's a tough lesson for those who've been taught to be so frugal and fair. It can make them more intolerant of the mistakes of others. And that sets them up for legalism; it opens them up to Pharisaism. We begin to look at our good and bad deeds as credits and debits, like money in the bank. We run the risk of turning salvation into an economic ledger. As long as we remain in the black, we're OK. Subconsciously, maybe we figure that we can save ourselves.

God's economy doesn't work like that. To Him, we're all hopelessly in debt. And *only through Him* can we be made rich.

It's a paradox of Christian life that the "better" we are, the harder it is to accept the truth of the gospel. The more we follow the rules, the more likely we'll miss the whole point.

I know how bad I've been—and am. I'm under no illusion that I can work my way to heaven. I know I need God's grace to carry me home. Better people than me need to come to understand the same thing. Compared to others, they may seem pretty decent. But in God's eyes, no one rises to the level of "decent" without His Son. Jesus didn't die to give us a little boost. He didn't come to earth because we could *almost* reach heaven, pretty good people that we are. He died to *save* us. We needed and continue to need saving.

We're all sinners. We're all broken. That's another reality we have to own. We have to accept the truth of our own brokenness and messiness. Only by seeing ourselves as God sees us can we ever hope to be made whole.

PART FOUR

The Family
of Memories

Chapter Ten

THE JOY OF
TOGETHERNESS

✦

Want to show your children humility? Buy an ATV or two. For me, I embarrassed myself even before I got on the thing.

We live in Colorado, a state full of forests, mountains, and, I've heard, millions of miles of all-terrain-vehicle-worthy trails. Take a few steps in the foothills, and you're bound to bump into a trail. Take a hike up to a lake, and vroom! ATVs will be everywhere. Listen to some ATV enthusiasts talk, and you'd think that the second you buy one of these recreational vehicles, the trails will practically clamor for your attention.

I experienced the opposite.

I felt pretty excited about buying a pair of ATVs—shiny, new, blue Polarises—for the family. We got a good deal on them, for one thing. They'd provide a nice excuse for our family to break away from the norm and explore the great state we live in, for another. But most importantly, I knew Trent and Troy would love 'em.

But after I got them, I realized something: I don't know anything about ATVs. I'm the poor kid from Compton, California. How would I know the first thing about these things?

But the only way to learn is to do, right? I'm an action-oriented guy. And since we live in a forested, foothill-laden part of the state,

I figured there had to be some trails pretty close to our house. In fact, I *knew* there would be. "Can't miss 'em," I was told.

But when I took the boys out to find them, I missed 'em. I couldn't find them anywhere. I drove everywhere, it seems, within an hour of our house, looking for those ATV trails. Nothing. The boys sat in the backseat, wondering whether their dad would wind up in Utah.

"Daaaaaad," came the call from the backseat.

"I know, I know," I said, a sense of failure welling up inside me. "I'm looking. I'm sorry."

We never found any trails. We wound up borrowing a friend's forty-acre backyard. That's where we broke in the Daly ATVs, vehicles that, when you watch the commercials on television, look like they can splash through any stream and climb every cliff face. And while the boys had a blast in our friend's backyard, I couldn't shake the thought that I'd failed them.

I swore I wouldn't make the same mistake next time. *We won't go ATVing in anyone's backyard this time,* I told myself. This time, we'd visit an area of the state *known* for its ATV trails, right around the Great Sand Dunes National Park in the southern part of the state. We were going down there anyway on a camping trip with Trent's Bible study group. We'd just stay an extra night, and when everyone else went home, the Dalys would rack up some hours on their almost-new ATVs—this time on *real* trails.

Or that was what I imagined anyway.

As the camping trip stretched on, however, I got a knot in my stomach, one that grew with each passing hour.

Listen, I'm the CEO of a worldwide ministry. I make tough decisions every day. I deal with angry advocates or miffed supporters more often than I would like. I get on national TV and take unpopular positions on the hottest of hot-button topics. I get hate mail. I've received death threats. Rarely does any of it faze me. But the prospect of not finding a stupid ATV trail, the possibility of disappointing my kids, terrified me.

Nature Calls

Ask Troy to name his favorite activity with the family, and he'll give a quick and unequivocal answer: camping.

I understand why.

It may sound strange to you, maybe counterintuitive. For many people, a good vacation includes fine restaurants. Spas. Real beds. Why would anyone take time off to "rough it"? What sort of sadist would give up steak dinners for charred hot dogs? Sleep-number beds for a glorified cot—or worse, a thin sleeping bag spread over the hard, cold ground? Or punt away heating and air conditioning for pure, unvarnished, unpredictable nature? Why?

But we love it. In the mountains and the deserts, away from the distractions of work, school, TV, and video games, something special happens. We talk more. We listen more. We laugh more. The noise of the everyday dies away. Weekday patterns recede. We remember who we are.

The home is supposed to be a safe place, but for our family, sometimes we need to leave the safety of home and get into a world populated with dangerous things. We need cliffs and rivers, heat and cold, bears and cougars and lots and lots of bugs, to really be us. We need this to get free of the expectations we put on ourselves and each other, to shed the stress that ties us up in knots.

For some enthusiasts, camping can be a cure for the curse of perfectionism. Nothing's perfect out there. Life is inherently messy—a dusty, sticky, hot, muggy, chilly, sappy, slimy, crusty mess. But somehow, we give ourselves permission to take joy in that mess, even to be a part of it. We don't fret over our hair. We don't worry about taking a shower every day (something for which the boys are grateful). We walk in the rain and laugh about it instead of running for shelter. We splash through a creek without worrying about ruining our shoes. We skin our knees. Scratch our bug bites. Wipe our runny noses on our sleeves.

Nature is God's country. He gave us the mountains and the

trees, the fish and the birds, the beauty and the mess. And you know what? He called it good. We gave ourselves air conditioning, shopping centers, sports cars, and credit cards—stuff designed to make us more comfortable, more attractive, more enviable. And we wonder why it all doesn't make us happier.

Living in this marvelous modern world of ours, we lose sight of what makes us truly happy. We get easily distracted. In our quest for our perfection, we forget about God's "good."

But sometimes, even out there in nature, we forget.

Getting Lost

The others in Trent's Bible study group had gone home. And so the Daly family started its quest for the ATV trails.

I'd looked up trails on the Internet and found a couple promising spots near Del Norte, just about an hour away. I felt *sure* we would run across some trails over there. Right?

But the trails, it seems, had gone into hiding. We didn't see anything. The boys remained pretty patient through the whole experience. They even started to offer suggestions. But I still couldn't shake the feeling that I was on the cusp of disappointing them.

Again.

"I'm sorry," I said, feeling a sense of déjà vu. "I'm really sorry!"

This, by the way, is my dirty little secret, my thing, my idol. While I don't expect my kids to be perfect, I do expect *me* to be. I want to live up to the "Greatest Dad Ever" label. I don't want to disappoint my kids. As a child, my fathers had let me down time after time after time. I promised myself I would turn out different. Better. I would never, *ever* let them down.

But there I was, letting them down.

My anxiety grew with each mile. The knot that formed in my stomach at the beginning of the camping trip seemed to fill up my whole body, shoving itself up into my throat. I saw a police officer by the side of the road, speed gun in hand, and I thought about interrupting him. *Hey*, I wanted to ask, *do you know where we might find an ATV trail around here? Somewhere where my fifteen- and thirteen-year-old boys can drive around? What? They need to be sixteen? Even if they're really mature for their ages?*

I thought better of asking the police officer.

Instead, I pulled over at a local convenience store and sidled up to the clerk. By this time, the quest for a good ATV trail felt like an unseemly quest, a secret that normal people weren't privy to. When I walked up to the girl behind the counter (she might have been eighteen), it almost had the vibe of a drug deal: *Pssst . . . you know where I can score me a trail suitable for all-terrain vehicles?*

Turns out she didn't, and I feared I would have to go back to my truck in shame. In that moment, I felt what it must feel like for Trent to turn over his report card to his mother when it has a D on it. I could already imagine the boys' disappointment and even scorn. I'd failed them yet again.

I felt a little sick.

But before I could turn and walk away, the girl mentioned that the guy who ran the coffee shop across the street might know. I bolted for the coffee shop and told him bluntly that I had no interest in coffee but really had to find some ATV trails.

"Sure," he said, "there's plenty right around here just 'bout twenty minutes down the road. Just take Highway 160 east and—"

Got it. His directions pointed us back to the very same campground we'd just left. Ironic.

Get Back to Where You Once Belonged

Broken families are a little like that. Sometimes we feel lost, like no path exists to get our families back to a healthy place. Sometimes when we've spent so many years trapped in our quest for perfection, when we've heaped so much scorn on our loved ones and shame on ourselves, it can seem impossible that anything'll ever be right again.

But sometimes we can find our way forward, out of our perfection traps and our aversion to messes, by going back. By remembering the better times, the fun times, the times when the family felt right . . . or at least better.

But what did those special times have in common?

Think back to the very beginning, when you held your child in your arms for the very first time.

That moment may have layers of unimagined complexity. New moms can feel strangely sad or full of an inexplicable angst. Moms and dads alike can feel a sense of relief or accomplishment. And many of us, in those first few moments when we hold that new life in our hands, may feel frightened. Unworthy. The anxiety and worry we feel may not be on our lips or in our thoughts, but they pound somewhere in our gut, in our souls. *I helped bring this life into the world,* the words tell us. *I hope I don't mess it up. I hope I'm a good parent.* If you're like me when Trent first found his way into my arms—this small, toothless miracle—you might've said a prayer: *Lord, help me. Lord, help me be a good parent. Help me be the best parent I can be.*

But we often feel something else, something more powerful, more primal than any other emotions roiling through our brains and bodies. Sometimes it can be the most powerful thing we've ever felt.

Love. Wonder. Joy. Something so powerful that words don't work. Something so strong that we laugh and cry and gasp in awe in the very same breath.

It's as if God wrapped heaven in a tiny body and gave it to us. It doesn't matter if he or she has scratches on its face or cradle cap. It doesn't matter what their future might hold—a childhood of unfettered success or constant challenge. Nothing matters except him. Her. And how blessed you are to be with your child right there, right then.

When we get married in a church, most of us take an oath before

God—to have and to hold, for richer, for poorer, in sickness and in health. We say a version of these words, and we mean them. But at the birth of a child, no oath is necessary. Most parents know, in the very core of their being, that just as nothing can separate us from the love of God, so nothing can separate our children from *our* love. No height, no depth, nothing present, nothing to come. Our love is unconditional. Our love is timeless. Until death do us part.

Now, think back to the most powerful memories you have of your child, whether they're six months old or sixteen years or even older. Recall their first steps. The time they ate their first piece of birthday cake. When they rode a bike. When they gave you flowers for your birthday. When they rode on your shoulders.

What do these moments share?

I bet when you think about these most critical memories, none of them involve a lot of words.

Sure, we can name exceptions. God designed us to communicate with others. Some of our most precious memories may include some deeply resonant phrases: "I love you." "I'm sorry." "You're my hero." And yes, even more action-oriented memories may have words connected to them. We may yell encouragement toward our daughter as she rides her bike for the first time, or praise our son after his violin recital. Laughter peppers a lot of our best memories.

But many of our deepest, most joyous moments need no words at all. Language is unnecessary. In fact, it's insufficient.

By contrast, the things that tend to tear down our families bit by bit, the things that break us, overflow with words.

"You're a failure."

"Why can't you behave?"

"That's not good enough."

When we look for perfection, we seek it through words. We instruct. We demand. We yell. We accuse. Even when we clam up, when we give our spouse or our children the silent treatment, our brains continue to work overtime, formulating our grievances, tabulating how we've been wronged, creating speeches and spreadsheets to illustrate just how far our loved ones have let us down.

I'm not knocking language. A big part of my job involves talking for a living, and we often have some very important things to say.

But when we look back on our most precious memories, the things that remind us of the love we have for each other, how many are lectures or discussions or diatribes? How many involve someone telling someone else how badly they're failing?

Not many, I imagine. In fact, I bet that lectures—ones we've given, ones we've received—often are the very things we'd most like to forget. Those moments can hurt us, shame us, and make us wish we were anywhere but where we are. When we aim to strengthen a family's bonds, words can sometimes get in the way.

And even the words we remember fondly—our dad teaching us how to work on the car, our mom walking us to the park for some fun—we tend to remember, not the words themselves, but the feeling of closeness we had just being with them. Whatever lessons we learned might have stuck with us. But when we remember the moment, it's not the words that resonate, but the voice. The smell. The sense of togetherness.

"Actions speak louder than words" goes the old cliché. But when we're patching up a breaking family or strengthening one that's already strong, it's true. Our actions speak for us, and often more eloquently and more powerfully than we could ever find the words for.

Linked Together

Jesus knew how much better we learn through action than through words. The Son of Man was a man of action Himself. He walked all over Judea, even in places where good Jewish men didn't go. He healed the blind. He raised the dead. The Bible doesn't tell us what Jesus told the five thousand people who gathered around Him one evening, but we know that somehow—with five loaves of bread and two fish—He fed them all (Mark 6:30–44). Sure, what He taught us is critically important, no question; but even then, Jesus often taught through parables. Most of His stories ring with action: a father throwing his prodigal son a party, a good Samaritan carrying a beaten traveler to an inn for caregiving, a shepherd rescuing a lost sheep.

Admittedly, I'm biased toward action. Jean is more of a formal, let's-sit-down-and-talk parent than I am. She likes to gather around the dining room table and have formal devotional times with the boys. But sometimes I think Trent and Troy find it hard to sit still long enough for anything to sink in. Or maybe that's just because I have a hard time sitting still myself.

When I want to talk with the boys, I like to talk while doing something else: we hike, we fish, maybe we play golf. Some of our best conversations have happened just driving to school. Men and boys, especially, like to focus parts of our minds on something totally different from the subject at hand. Our thoughts click a little easier; our words flow a little more readily. Maybe when the body is at work, the mind knows it can kick back and relax a little. And a relaxed mind, I believe, makes for a more receptive mind.

Different environments can reinforce what we want to tell our children too. In Africa, Troy seemed particularly struck by the poverty he saw. I asked him at one point, "Have you considered why God put you where He put you? Why He put your spirit into this body? Put you in our family? Put us all in this country of ours with all its many blessings?" I wanted him to think about that for a little bit. Our lives could've turned out much different. And while I could've asked him the very same question in a heart-to-heart back home, it impacted him more, surrounded by the need and the poverty and these clamoring, joyful children.

But did I even need to ask him at all? For him to see Zambia for himself, to meet these kids, spoke far more eloquently than I could have. He'll remember that trip for the rest of his life. We all will.

Memories

In one of my previous books, *The Good Dad*, I suggested that our shared experiences help forge links between us and our children—bonds that, we hope, can't be broken. I suggested it looked a little like a tetherball. Imagine you're the pole and your child is the ball. A rope or tether connects you two—made of your shared affection and love. Each memory you create together has an impact on that tether. The bad ones may weaken or fray it, but the good ones strengthen it. Each strand of memory we make—a baseball game, a trip to Yellowstone, the school play we praise our child for participating in—gets added to the tether, making the bonds between mother and child, father and child, stronger and more resilient. Accumulate enough of these memories, and the tether will become almost impossible to break, no matter what rough spots may lie ahead.

And what if that tether has already grown weaker than you'd like? What if it's frayed through constant arguments or our collective drive for perfection? What if we've spent too much time in our families cutting down our family members and ourselves, telling each other we're not good enough? When families get stressed and anxious over outsized expectations, they can find it hard to turn things around.

When a family environment gets too poisoned, it can seem like everything we say to each other, even when said with the best of intentions, just makes it worse. Every word can sound like an accusation. Every sentence threatens to make someone angry or defensive. It can seem like every conversation, no matter how much we wish it otherwise, frays the tether just a little more.

In times like these, we have to follow Jesus' example. We have to remember that our actions can communicate far much more eloquently than words can. So put the lectures on the back burner; shove to the side all the recriminations, justified or not. Even when you know you'll *need* to have some difficult conversations later, sometimes we just have to close our mouths, open our eyes, and make some memories. We have to remember what's good and wonderful about being together. Sometimes the only sound we need to hear is the swish of a basketball net. The chirping of crickets during an early-evening walk. The soft thud of nails pounded in a birdhouse.

Or in my case, the growl of an engine.

Trailing Off

We finally found the ATV trail. We roared through the brush in Alamosa's sandy, sage-filled foothills and had a great time.

Or at least most of us did.

The knot in my stomach that day never really left. I never reached a point where I could really let go. *I don't know what I'm doing*, I thought. *I'm such a loser. It took me too long to find this place. We wasted so much time . . .*

But that anxiety, that quest for perfection, didn't transfer to Trent and Troy.

Trent had endured a rough year in school. His mom and I had been on his case constantly, trying to keep him on track. Life at home for all three of us had grown pretty stressful. Lots of talk about grades and homework. It probably seemed to Trent that every time Jean or I talked to him, we'd talk about school. What he wasn't doing. What he *should* be doing. Why he wasn't good enough.

But out there, on that ATV, you could almost see all the stress just fall off his shoulders. You could see him relax. No one quizzed him about his grades. He didn't worry about showing Jean and me his latest algebra quiz or fret about getting his homework done. That afternoon, only one thing was on his mind: riding that ATV. I could see him handle the thing with grace and confidence. When we stopped for a minute or two to switch up, I could see his smile and sense his energy and excitement. He didn't need to tell us he was having a good time; we could feel it.

He was himself that afternoon. More than that, he was his best self.

Sometimes the expectations we put on each other, justified or not, can feel like chains pulling us down. And when we can put those chains down, even for an afternoon, we feel so much stronger, so much better. Even though I couldn't manage to drop my own set of chains, Trent did. And you could tell the difference.

More importantly, we created a memory that afternoon. We put another strand on the tether.

Trent is sixteen now. As I write, he'll be going into his sophomore year of high school, tackling a new slate of classes, meeting new teachers, and, once more, dealing with another set of expectations, another set of pressures.

Neither of us know what the coming year will bring for him. I'm sure he's going into it with the best of intentions, but neither of us can say for sure whether all those good intentions will turn into positive results. We don't know whether our discussions about grades are in the past or whether we're looking at another stressful year.

But even if we run into some of those same issues, I know we'll survive it. Because even when we fight, we've got a few things locked down: Trent knows that Jean and I want only what's best for him. I know that, no matter what struggles he may have at times, his heart and character are solid. The tether between us is strong. And the memories we create and the time we spend together creating them make it only stronger.

Chapter Eleven

TRANSITIONS

✦

Whem Yuma Hasegawa celebrated his twentieth birthday on October 4, 2015, his parents gave him an extra-special present: a resignation letter.

"Notice of Expiration of Child-Rearing Services," the note announced in Japanese. "Going forward, please become a proper and responsible member of society, like your father and mother. In addition, should you continue living in the Hasegawa family home, please make a monthly payment of 20,000 yen [US$168] for rent, utility, and grocery expenses. Also, please be aware that should you ask for a loan from your parents, interest will be charged."[1]

The note was all in good fun. Yuma Hasegawa had already been paying rent to his parents. But the note illustrates a fallacy that many parents harbor going into momhood and dadhood—in fact, *there is no expiration date.*

Maybe we assume that our duties end when our kids turn eighteen and finish high school. Maybe it's twenty-two, when they graduate from college. Maybe it's somewhere in between. But we imagine a line exists between childhood (when parents run the show and call the shots) and adulthood (when our kids become wholly responsible for their own lives, and your parental duties shrink to just cooking the family turkey for Thanksgiving).

But childhood doesn't work like that. Maybe it never has, and it certainly doesn't anymore. It seems that puberty is eating away at both childhood and adulthood, beginning sometimes when our kids are nine or ten and lasting into their late twenties. Most parents don't write resignation letters; they work overtime. And they find themselves forced to deal with adolescence—a critical, painful time of angst, tension, school-based stress, and massive transitions—for a lot longer.

Kids really do hit puberty earlier. By the time they enter late elementary school, they're forced—by school, the culture, and often their own parents—to be smarter and more focused than we ever were at their age. By the time middle school comes, they and their parents may already be planning for college. And so they watch their GPAs, sweat over tests, cry over C's, and participate in scads of extracurricular activities to catch somebody's eye at Yale. The quest for perfection starts early.

In the midst of all this school-based stress, our children get exposed to more of the culture's crassness and filth than ever before. Language formerly the domain of sailors has become normal banter in the schoolroom cafeteria. At an age when most of us parents were working up the courage to hold somebody's hand, our children may feel pressured to send out into cyberspace naked pictures of themselves. According to a 2014 study by Drexel University, more than half of the college students they surveyed had sent or received sexually explicit texts or images before they turned eighteen.[2]

And if you think that Christian, churchgoing families are immune, think again.

Meanwhile, *adult* children are taking their time to embrace all the responsibilities of adulthood. Scientists say that our kids' brains don't become fully formed until about age twenty-five, and for some, that's just the *beginning* of getting out on their own. They're getting married later. They stick around home longer. In fact, in 2014, more millennials, young adults between the ages of eighteen and thirty-four, were still living with their parents than were married and out on their own—the first time in *130 years* that has been the case!

Growing up in the twenty-first century has become such a mysterious, anxiety-riddled process that millennials have coined a new verb to describe it: *adulting*.

These trends could be symptoms of everything we've talked about in this book, including the pressure that parents put on their kids to never fail, which leads to more stress and anxiety in school. All that pressure, all the worries about not being good enough, leads them to seek love and affirmation elsewhere, even if it means snapping nude pics of themselves. Ironically, that very same pressure can create a culture of overabundant caution. They worry so much about failure that they feel afraid to make big decisions and take big leaps on their own.

When they're thirteen, our children want to grow up right now. By the time they're twenty-one, they're afraid to. It seems an entire generation has gotten stuck at age seventeen.

And maybe as parents we should sympathize more. After all, growing up is *tough*. While we want the freedom, the responsibilities that go with it can be a bear.

We mature by increments. We don't magically "grow up" when we turn eighteen or twenty-one. It doesn't happen when we get our driver's license or take our first legal drink of beer or vote for the very first time. And a lot of times, that process isn't particularly fun—for children or their parents. It's filled with transitions, and every transition will come with its share of pain.

Many parents, and probably a lot of kids, try to avoid these transitions for as long as possible. We like to keep things comfortable. Secure. Neat. Transitions, after all, can be pretty messy. But as much as we may kick and scream, they'll come anyway. We all have to grow up sometime. And if we don't, then we land in a different world of hurt.

But how do you navigate these transitions without moving to a state of insanity? By being firm. By being flexible. And maybe most importantly, by allowing yourself to be fallible.

Setting Boundaries

From the moment our kids start toddling around the house on their own shaky little legs, parents start putting up boundaries. At first the boundaries are physical. We put our children in playpens. We put baby gates across stairways. We make sure always to close the door to the backyard. As time goes on, we start slapping up boundaries in other areas of their lives too. *You can't have dessert till you finish your dinner. You can't play video games until your homework's done. You can't stay up past 9:00 p.m. on a school night.*

These rules are important. Just like a playpen or the baby gates, they set the perimeter for where and when your children can safely, comfortably roam, whether physically, spiritually, or culturally.

Even as our boys grow older, Jean and I take their boundaries seriously. We keep a close eye on the games Trent and Troy play and the movies they watch. We want to make sure they don't stay out with friends until all hours. They don't do many sleepovers.

For years, we didn't even let them have cell phones, a move that some kids would consider cruel and unusual. Even as most of their friends got phones, we held firm. When they'd ask—and they would periodically—we'd tell them, "No, we're not there yet. We think they're too dangerous for you guys."

They'd accept our decision with good grace. "OK," they'd say. Trent even told Troy one time that they may as well give up. "Troy, we're probably not going to get phones until we're sixteen and driving," he said, "so just live with it." And he said it just like a parent might. His words impressed me.

(They do have phones now, by the way. I kind of unilaterally opened that door about a year ago in Disneyland, just so we could keep in touch with them. I got them both cheap little flip phones with no Internet access. Neither of them were driving yet, but they weren't far off.)

That's the thing about good, solid boundaries: Once they know where they are, and if you consistently enforce them, most kids will accept them with only a token grumble or two. Those boundaries become like well-placed baby gates: No matter how you cry or shake your fists, they aren't coming down. So you go on to other things.

But baby gates don't stay up forever. As your child grows, the shape of the boundaries needs to change. And sometimes parents, desperate to control their kids and cut down on the messes, are slow to change them. We forget that our kids will eventually have to create their own boundaries. The teen years can be a good time to give them some practice.

When Trent turned fourteen, and I mean *the day* he turned fourteen, I was driving him to school when I said, "Trent, can you believe that next year you're going to have your permit? You're going to be driving!" *Crazy*, I thought. *It didn't seem all that long ago that I was able to swing Trent around by his arms. Now he's growing like a weed and on the verge of being a high school freshman with a driver's permit.*

But I wanted to dig a little bit deeper. I wanted to remind him about the freedoms and responsibilities, and the boundaries, that come with it.

"Let me ask you a question," I said. "I just had people on the broadcast who decided not to set a hard, fast curfew with their kids. The dad just sat down his children—a teenage boy and girl—and instructed them just to come home at 'a reasonable hour.'

"Well, the girl always came home way earlier than she needed to. Had there been a curfew, it would've been set a couple hours later than his daughter ever got home. But his son always showed up far, far later. For him, a reasonable hour seemed like one or two in the morning. So eventually the dad had to change the rules for his son. And he had to take the keys away to teach his boy to come home earlier.

"Now how would that work for you?" I asked Trent. "When you get your driver's license, is this something you'd want us to do? Or would you rather have a hard, firm curfew?"

Trent laughed.

"I'd probably rather have a firm time," he told me. "I'd rather know what the boundary is."

That may sound like a pretty innocuous conversation, but I hope it did at least a couple of things.

First, it got Trent to thinking about what sort of person he is in regard to boundaries. Does he deal better with hard boundaries or soft ones? Can he trust himself with a nebulous, "reasonable" guideline? Or is he the kind of guy who'd be more inclined to push? I already knew the answer. Trent likes to push. But it's one thing for *me* to see it, and another thing for Trent to see that for himself. When we understand ourselves, we're well on our way to figuring out how to be good, wise, productive adults. Through understanding ourselves, we learn to set our own boundaries that can curb our own weaknesses.

The conversation also opened an important door. I was inviting him to help Jean and me set his own boundaries. When your kids feel as though they have some say in the boundaries you set, they'll be more likely to follow them. If they helped you choose an 11:00 p.m. curfew, two weeks later they won't rail about how unfair that curfew is.

We need to remember that parenthood isn't about protecting a set of arbitrary rules; it's about helping your kids grow into strong, wise, caring adults. Early on in a child's life, your rules and boundaries help them learn what that looks like and point them in the right direction—you treat elders with respect; you finish the work you said you were going to do, etc. But as your children grow and as you give them the opportunity to shape their own boundaries, they take on an expanded role. Instead of leading them by the hand to what they *should* do—that is, what you want them to do—you can walk alongside them more, guiding them when necessary, but having to guide them less and less.

To be an adult means setting your own boundaries. It means making your own decisions, even if the decisions don't always turn out for the best (or please Mom and Dad).

Taking Risks

In the summer of 2016, the Daly family took our ATVs to Zion National Park. While you can't use the vehicles inside the park, plenty of trails and places to ride them exist outside. We used those trails a lot.

I let Troy drive one of the ATVs through some nearby sand dunes, and he went pretty fast (yes, we had helmets on . . . that's mandatory). I was on the back, holding on. We spun around, covering ground at a pretty good clip, and suddenly, in front of us, I saw the lip of a dune rapidly approaching. It was a high lip, and there was no way either of us could see anything on the other side. That lip might've hidden just another stretch of sand, or it might've concealed a ledge or a dry river embankment or, who knows, a huge cliff. I mean, this was wild, scenic Utah after all. You never know when a canyon might just suddenly pop up out of nowhere.

I thought about asking Troy to slow down, but it was too late. We were going too fast. In a heartbeat we hit the lip of the dune and went *flying*—wheels spinning, engine whining. If someone had videotaped us, they might've used it in an ATV commercial (as long as they did something about the look of fear plastered across my face). I'm sure we looked impressive.

FOOM!

We landed upright. Troy skidded to a stop. We looked back at the tracks and saw—I kid you not—fifteen feet of unmarred sand from the point where we took off to the point where we landed.

"Troy, dude!" I said.

"Yeah," he said from behind his helmet. "Sorry. That was a little fast."

Remember how I said that as time goes on, we want to get in a position to walk beside our children instead of leading them? Maybe guiding them with a helpful word or two? Well, let me amend that: Sometimes as our kids go through those transitions from childhood to adulthood, it doesn't always feel as if we're walking quietly, gently alongside them. Sometimes it can feel like I'm riding with Troy, clinging to the child as he barrels along, hoping both of us won't die.

Troy has always had an abundance of confidence. "Stupid courage," I'd call it.

That confidence shows up in more positive, less heart-stopping ways too. Both of my boys play football, and Troy is always the guy to pat the other guys on the helmet and slap them on the back. "Good job!" he'll say. "Way to go!" He'll run over to the pile and pick people up. A certain courage goes along with that rah-rah attitude, that confidence to encourage your teammates. I played my share of football in high school, and I don't think I ever did much of that. I just felt too overwhelmed thinking about the next play I needed to call as quarterback. I felt nervous most of the time. But little rattles Troy. He already has the feel of a leader to me, and leaders inherently have to be risk takers.

Trent, meanwhile, has his own sort of confidence. He may not barrel off the lip of a sand dune, like Troy would. He's more calculated about his risk taking. He would have driven to the top of the dune and looked down the other side. Trent's confidence centers on his ability to think. He has a good head on his shoulders and knows how to use it. He's a natural debater, is very strong-willed, and will rarely back down from an intellectual or argumentative challenge, even when he should.

Both of our children take risks in their own ways. And on some level, that's exactly what a parent wants. I've said before that growing up in a safe home, one where the kids know that their moms and dads have their backs, gives them a license to be daring. To take chances. To live the full, purposeful life that God wants us to live. Both of our boys seem to be leaders in their own ways. Troy is the backslapper, the encourager, the social one. Trent's strong mind and strong will make him more of an idealist. I imagine King David probably was that kind of kid. Joseph too. Firm. Stubborn, even. God creates people like that for a special purpose, and Jean and I have both said that if Trent stays on the good side, God will use his special leadership ability.

But when they're in the midst of that transition, deciding what kind of person they want to be and beginning to make decisions on their own, we parents can wonder whether our kids will stick to the good side. When our children take risks and define their own character through those risks, it's hard for parents to sit back and relax.

Troy is doing fine, but I still worry that, because he's so affable and so eager to please, and because he's not really afraid of taking physical risks, he may be a little more prone to peer pressure. He may get pulled through a harmful door. He may take risks in college that Jean and I would rather he didn't take.

I don't worry about that with Trent. I'm confident that when he leaves the house, no one will talk him into doing *anything* he doesn't want to do. That mind-set, of course, brings its own share of challenges. He's more likely to say or do something that might offend somebody—pop off to someone on the college football team, for instance, or give a little lip to the boss.

If that happens, though, I think it'll be ultimately good for him. Life may humble him a little, because life has a way of humbling us all.

Wash Your Hands

We've already talked about the importance of letting our children take responsibility for their own decisions. They need to own their choices. In times of transition, however, we parents don't worry only about their choices; we worry about their attitudes, their whole outlook on life. We worry that the way they act, talk, and even the way they *think* might hurt them or hold them back. We worry that when they hit that lip of the sand dune, they'll get hurt.

And you know what? We might be right. Their risks, whatever those risks look like, may lead to hurt. Their attitudes may leave them open to failure or being made a fool of. We don't want that to happen to our precious children!

But as a parent, you can't squeeze that youthful confidence out of your child, no matter how it manifests itself. You can't talk them out of their penchant for risk taking. You can't lecture away their poor attitudes. It's not our job; it's *life's* job.

Because, let's face it, most of us have been there.

A friend of mine was talking with his twenty-four-year-old son-in-law the other night. The son-in-law said, "You know, when I was eighteen, I thought I knew *everything*."

Most of us think we know everything when we're eighteen or twenty-two or twenty-four. Our parents can seem like the most clueless people on the face of the planet. But then life happens. It humbles us. It tempers us. The sharp, wild abandon and the headstrong confidence we had begin to soften. As the months and years go by, our parents look smarter. They still may not have any idea what to do with Snapchat, but when it comes to the lasting lessons they tried to teach, the stuff that remains relevant year after year, decade after decade, our kids come to appreciate those lessons. Your son or daughter isn't always going to be, as Kevin Leman would say, "a stupid teenager."

But as a parent yourself, it can be hard to wait for that stupidity to evaporate. Even parents who've never so much as spanked their child have strong urges to knock some sense into them when they become teenagers.

It's ironic. At an age when we should be loosening our grip on our kids, we often ratchet down on them instead. Our volume goes up. Our punishments get more extreme. We feel desperate to make our kids change. Time is running out!

When I look inside my own home and family, however, it doesn't seem like this strategy is working. All that high-intensity stress, all those demands we pile on, don't make things better. Often, they seem to make the situation worse. We don't just have a kid struggling with homework; we have a *stressed, anxious, angry* kid struggling with homework (along with an angry mom and dad). Instead of standing back and saying, "Hey, this isn't working; maybe we should try something new," we double down on all the stress and reinforce all our demands. We plant our parental flag on the hill and refuse to move, because we know *we're right*. But why not be a little more pragmatic about it all and try to find *what works*? As a frequent guest on the Focus on the Family broadcast, Cynthia Tobias often says, "What's the point?"

Do you know what a "stay the course" attitude often leads to? Losing our children. They drift away from us an argument at a time. We shame. We demean. Right in the middle of these teen transitions, when our children are desperately trying to figure out what it means to be an adult, we treat them like children. We stop listening. We keep lecturing. And they begin to slip away. The unproductive fights put another brick between us. Snap another thread of the tether. *I don't need this*, they think. Because who does?

Sometimes I think I can even feel those tether threads snap. I can see them in our children's eyes.

On Trial

Trent's grades spark another round of lecturing. Arguing. All of us have been here before. We recite our lines by heart.

And then, in the midst of the fighting and finger-pointing, the blame and the anger, we make eye contact.

Help me, he seems to say. *Defend me. I know I'm not perfect. But be my dad. Be my dad. I'm dying.*

And it catches me. I'm paralyzed. I don't know what to do.

Defend me. I'm dying.

What are parents? They're teachers. Counselors. CEOs. Janitors. But unfortunately, particularly when raising teens in transition, we sometimes become lawyers. Not judges, fair and impartial arbiters of justice, sitting on the bench and weighing the evidence. We become prosecuting attorneys, pointing fingers at the accused and pushing for jail time. Justice isn't blind in many homes; it's biased toward the prosecution, where those bringing the charges and those making the verdict are two and the same—Mom and Dad. And the child accused sits alone, defending himself. *Out of order. Overruled. Don't talk back to the judge.*

Maybe—I hope—justice still can be served in those environments. At least, most of the time.

But I find it interesting that when the Bible delves into courtroom metaphors, it's Satan who serves as the prosecuting attorney.

The very word *devil* is rooted in the Greek word translated "accuser." The Hebrew term *ha-satan* can be interpreted as "the prosecutor." No wonder that in the Old Testament, Satan often seems to serve as a prosecuting lawyer in God's heavenly courtroom. In the King James Version of Psalm 109:6, the psalmist seems ready to hire Lucifer himself to prosecute his enemies: "Set thou a wicked man over him: and let Satan stand at his right hand."

And where does Jesus stand in God's courtroom? By our side.

"My dear children, I write this to you so that you will not sin," we read in 1 John 2:1. "But if anybody does sin, we have an advocate with the Father—Jesus Christ, the Righteous One."

Throughout this book, I've encouraged us as parents to model ourselves after Jesus. He loves. He is filled with grace. And when the chips are down, He doesn't stand against us, wagging a finger; He *defends* us.

Maybe we parents could learn from that as well. When our children stand accused of some home-based violation, is it possible we're not always called to be both judge and prosecution, but judge and defense? To be an advocate in our own court for our own child?

It may be.

But how do you fill this role? How can you protect the rule of law while defending the accused lawbreaker?

The answer goes right back to some of our fundamentals.

You have to follow the Golden Rule. Is that how you'd like to be treated if the roles were reversed?

You have to take the time to listen, really listen, to what your transitioning teen has to say. Take the time to learn their side of the story. Sometimes there are extenuating circumstances. Sometimes deeper things are at play inside the conflict. Is it really just a matter of not getting the homework done, or is it a symptom of a deeper problem? Not enough sleep or trouble in school or even a festering issue between her and you?

Talk through the issue, calmly and gently, so they understand your side too. Through the art of talking and listening, a lot of fights can be defused and a lot of workable solutions found.

Be Honest

Boundaries. Risks. Grace. All of these are critical elements in raising kids to become healthy, thriving adults. They're particularly critical during times of transition, when family life can get even messier than usual.

But we need to talk about one more area, one we overlook at our peril: the importance of being honest. Not honest about our taxes or our work or how we *really* feel about Grandma's tuna-chocolate casserole, but honest about ourselves.

You know how dogs can sense fear? Children, teens especially, can sense hypocrisy. Trent in particular has a nose for this. And when they're teens, they'll call you out on your inconsistency.

It goes back to one of our fundamentals. You have to be the example you want to see. You can't pretend. If you want your teen's respect, you have to earn it. And more than anything, teens respect honesty and transparency. They don't expect perfection from us. They really don't! So don't pretend to be perfect.

Easy, right? No, not really. It's harder than it sounds.

We've already acknowledged it can be difficult to expose our imperfections to our children. But with teens, it can become even harder. They already know everything, remember? They think we know nothing. Since it's only natural that we want to prove them wrong, we tend to overcompensate. We hide our weaknesses, ignore our mistakes. And in our effort to keep our kids' respect, we wind up losing it.

So don't fake it. Own up to your weaknesses. Apologize when you make a mistake. Most importantly, be appropriately honest about your past. When your teens are failing, acknowledge when you've failed in that area too.

Think of this honesty, this transparency about yourself, a little like drip irrigation. No, you don't want to let all of your deep, dark childhood secrets spill out all at once. I wouldn't cut off the end of the hose and let all that ugly history gush out! But don't cut off the water of wisdom altogether. When you don't show your weaknesses, when you pretend to your children that you're something other than human, you risk cutting off the water altogether. You won't nourish your relationship with your kids, and they won't grow.

So let the truth drip out a little bit at a time, depending on the circumstance and the age of the child. One, it allows your children to see you in a different, healthier light. It lets them see that you're not perfect either and you need grace, forgiveness, and patience just like they do. Two, it reminds you that *you're* not perfect. It forces you into a position where, just like your child, you can use a little grace—and it makes it easier for you to give a little of that grace too. To show that imperfection *isn't* a weakness, as much as we might think it is. It *doesn't* undercut our authority, even though sometimes we imagine it does. No, every opportunity we have to water that soil—to say to our kids, "I'm not perfect, and neither are you"—is a good thing. It waters our relationship. It helps our children grow, to stretch their roots into the soil.

Parenting beyond the Transition

Our trip to Zion National Park in Utah wasn't just about hiking and driving our ATVs around. We had a lot of hanging-out time too. It was hot when we drove out there—temperatures in the nineties or hundreds all the time. But our campsite was surrounded by big shade trees. We sat underneath our RV's long awning. We'd just sit outside, sip cold drinks, and talk.

Troy and I talked quite a bit during that trip. We talked about the foster kids who were playing in the dirt in front of us. We talked some about how he's doing spiritually and how he's doing in other ways. You could say we watered our own relationship. In that hot, dry climate, we helped something grow a little bit stronger, a little bit greener.

In ten years, that's what I hope Troy and I will still be doing. In twenty years, God willing. Even in thirty.

That's what parenthood becomes after a while. You stop keeping your kids away from the hot stove. You're not teaching them how to ride a bike. You don't worry about their messy rooms or their bad grades. You talk. You share. You give advice. I already lean this way with my boys, when I can. That's my mentality. They're old enough to own their decisions, own their mistakes. But if they need my help, my advice, I'm here. "You can take it or leave it," I say—"but if I were you, I'd take it."

I look forward to the day when that's what fatherhood looks like all the time. I think it's my natural bent. I'm an advice giver. Granted, this parenting style doesn't work well with young children. But when they grow older, in their later teens and transitioning into adulthood and even beyond, it works. Once they're grown, in fact, it's the only thing that does.

Imperfect parenting pays off right here. You've allowed your children to make messes. You've treated their mistakes with grace. You've openly and honestly talked with them about your own imperfections.

You've watered that garden and strengthened that tether. You've preserved your relationship with your children, and now *they* come to *you*—not so you can kiss a boo-boo or give them money, but to talk. To ask questions. To relax with you. To laugh with you. To feel that safe place of *home*, even as they begin building a home of their own.

Letting Go

What does the Christian walk of faith look like? For many of us, it's a journey of relinquishment. We give up a little bit of ourselves every day, every year. We die to ourselves so we can be reborn into something a little closer to the person God wants us to be.

In a way, I think the same can be said of parenting. It's a journey of relinquishment. It's a long lesson in letting go.

Our children know nothing when they come to us. We have total control over their tiny lives. As the years go by, we give them whatever knowledge of wisdom they possess. We teach them to stand, to walk, to ride a bike, to fly.

But with each new step they take, each new lesson they learn, we loosen our grip a little. We take our hands away from them in the pool and let them float. We let go of the bicycle seat and let them roar down the road.

And somewhere along the line, the reality of what we're doing smacks us straight in the forehead. We're teaching them to leave us.

No wonder our expectations are so high! No wonder we demand so much! No wonder those teenage years can be so hard, so angry!

We remember what it was like to hold that child in our arms. We remember the promises we made. We remember that when we were with our daughters and sons—when they laughed as we threw them in the air, when they held our hands as we crossed a street, when they fell asleep as we read to them—we felt whole. We felt loved in a way that maybe we've never felt before. In those moments, we felt closer to the men and women we should be, the men and women God wants us to be.

We felt . . . *perfect.*

To let go means letting that illusion go too. When we let go, we're telling ourselves that we've done the best we can with our children. We're sending them off, imperfect though they may be. And if they're not perfect, neither are we.

We let go, even though we want more time. We want another chance. We want to feel that feeling again.

We let go, understanding that we're relinquishing control. "Thy will be done," we say.

But God loves paradox. He tells us that when we lose our lives, we save them. He tells us that His foolishness is wiser than our wisdom. Through Christ, He showed us that the King of the universe can be a child born in a stable; that the most glorious victory can look like defeat.

And when we finally let go—let go of our perfect expectations, let go of blame, let go of all the things that hold us back as parents, and, finally, when we let go of our children to become men and women, husbands and wives, fathers and mothers—they come back.

God willing, they come back.

We never resign our jobs as parents. We're moms and dads for life, with no guarantees. No safety nets, no promises. God's plan and our own choices can overturn even perfect parenting. We can do everything right, and yet our children can go wrong. We can fail our children, and yet they can still succeed despite us.

But the time comes to let go, the time to say good-bye. And we simply have to trust, hope, and pray that the good-bye opens the door for a life of new hellos, that our grown sons and daughters will put their hand in ours again, squeeze it, and smile.

They'll be in your arms again, and you in theirs. This is home. This is whole. And God will say to you, "Well done."

Chapter Twelve

THE BEST FAMILY

◆

I learned about family between commercials.

The Brady Bunch. Family Affair. My Three Sons. That was what family looked like to me. Not the messy, fractured family I lived with—the hardworking, hardly-ever-there mom; the drunk, abusive dad; the strict, overbearing stepdad. On television, I saw what family should be. Loving parents. Obedient children. Problems solved every thirty minutes. Every episode ends in a punch line.

Families don't look like that. I know that now. You do too.

But I wonder. How many of us are still trying to live up to that ideal? How many of us, in the deepest parts of our soul, are still looking for that perfect family?

Regrets

Ask Trent and Troy what advice *they'd* give parents, what they think is the most important thing moms and dads should concentrate on with their own children, and they'll give two very different answers.

"Boundaries," Troy will say. "You can't have boundaries so tight that you can't have a childhood, but they need to be there. You need boundaries to get them in the right direction."

So says Troy, the kid who always wants to be in the right; the kid who does his homework; the kid who wonderfully wants to please us each and every day. He flourishes under boundaries. He excels when he knows the rules. He follows them so well.

"I would tell them to listen," says Trent. "You should listen to them. Just hear what they have to say. I think a lot of parents just kind of pull the discipline card without ever hearing their kids' side."

Why do parents struggle to listen sometimes?

"I think it's difficult, because they *think* they know what's going on," Trent says. "They were a teen too, so they think they understand. But that's not always the case." The world has changed a lot since most parents were teens. *My Three Sons* has given way to vaping and sexting, Facebook and Netflix. It's a bewildering world out there, and parents don't always get it.

But listening isn't just about gaining a better understanding of what your children are dealing with. It's about, Trent says, making the child feel loved and supported. It's about creating a safe place.

"When you listen, the child feels like you're definitely there for them," Trent says.

The Daly family has done well with our boundaries. We gave Trent plenty when he was younger. We were hard on him: *Stand up, sit down. Spit, don't spit. Smile, don't smile.* We had high expectations for him and for us.

But how well have we listened?

We grade our children all the time. We might not give them letter grades or slap a gold star on their progress reports, but nearly every day we grade them on their rooms. Their work. Their attitude. "Good job," we say. "Needs improvement," we say.

But turnabout is fair play. Regularly, I ask Trent and Troy to grade me. Am I getting an A? a B? an F?

Usually they give me A's or B's. They're pretty generous with me in that regard, although I don't know I deserve it. When Trent or Troy say, "You're a great dad," I want to believe them, but I'm not sure I do.

I get angry when I shouldn't get angry. I belittle and blame and lecture when I should listen. All the things I say parents should avoid doing, I've done. I still do them.

Some days I wonder whether I've simply talked my kids into thinking I'm a great father. I wonder whether I've fooled myself into believing it.

"You're not perfect, Jim," Jean will tell me. And she's right. But am I even good?

I'm an older dad. I'll be fifty-eight when Troy leaves the house. So I sometimes wonder what the kids will say about me when I'm gone. I wonder what they'll say at my funeral.

"My dad was funny," they'll say. They always say that even when I'm around. "My dad has a great sense of humor."

But you know what I really want them to say?

"He was the best dad I ever could've had." And I want it to be real.

I don't want to be a hypocrite. I want to be the dad who my children needed me to be.

I worry they won't be able to say that. I worry there was a disconnect between the dad I thought I was, the dad I wanted to be, and the dad they knew and saw.

Parents so often hurt their children. Close friends of mine have worked for years, even decades, on healing the wounds inflicted by their mothers and fathers. How many psychiatrists and counselors owe their livelihoods to moms and dads who just didn't get it? Too many, I fear. Greg, one of my good buddies from my high school basketball team, probably got thrown out of more games for fighting than he played. He seemed angry all the time. Why? He had a terrible relationship with his father. Only after he became a Christian was he able to reconcile with his dad and begin to heal and live a healthier life.

I never want Trent or Troy to look back on their childhood and see that kind of relationship with me. I don't want them to look back in their twenties and somehow have to reconcile all this anger rooted in their relationship with me. But honestly, I think the possibility exists. I'm doing everything I can to avoid it, but am I doing enough? Am I giving enough? Am I *good enough*?

Chasing Grace

In my boyhood home, milkshakes sometimes took the place of my mom. My home was where the police came to haul away my drunk, cursing dad. My home was where, night after night, the only stability in sight was *The Brady Bunch*.

Trent and Troy's home looks much different. Jean and I have worked hard to make it so. It has a loving mother and father, structure, love, fun. Stability. Take a picture, and we're all smiles. We look pretty great . . . if you don't look too closely.

An editor of a prominent family magazine once said that, ironically, his best "parenting" writers weren't parents. These writers could confidently ply readers with expert advice without the messy reality of parenthood getting in the way. Answers that seem so obvious in the abstract aren't so easy in the midst of the mess.

I work for a ministry dedicated to family. I talk with the world's greatest marriage and parenting experts. Millions of families look to the organization I lead, seeking advice and answers.

Truth is, I don't have "satisfaction guaranteed or your money back" answers. For all the advantages we have, all the advice I've been given, all the familial perks that come with my job, I'm looking for answers too. My family is messy sometimes, just like yours. My family struggles, just like yours. Honestly, my family sometimes feels as though it's cracked and broken. I can feel like a failure.

But in that brokenness, our families are made whole. In that hurt, we heal.

What is a family? It's all the things we've talked about, and more.

It's home. It's work. It's school. It's the people you love more than anyone. It's the people who can hurt you more deeply than you thought possible. It's memories, both good and bad. It's our foundation for the future, for better or worse.

And it's God's. His design, His plan, His tool to help us deal with this fractured, fallen world, even though the family itself is just as fractured and fallen.

We want our families to be perfect because we know that's what they *should* be. They should be places of love and learning, hope and promise. Safe places. Happy places.

They should be Eden . . . but they're not. When the world fell, the family fell. We're outside the walls. In Genesis, God gave Eve the pain of childbirth. And in our families, we feel that pain still.

Right There

Sarah and Eric watched poolside as their seven-year-old daughter, Heather, stood at the edge of the water. Square tiles spelled out the depth: "10 FT." But to Heather, the pool must've looked bottomless. She stood at the edge, her arms wrapped protectively around her middle, shaking her head vigorously as her teacher implored her, *begged* her, to jump.

If my dad had been in the pool, he might've yanked her into the water. But no one here would do that to Heather. Everyone waited as she stood, shaking from cold.

Sarah had known that Heather would struggle. Before today's lesson, mother and daughter had talked about it, Sarah even offering a bribe—ice cream afterward—for a good, brave jump. But the promise of Rocky Road wasn't enough. Her little girl still shuffled her feet by the pool, a line of other swimmers impatiently waiting their turn.

Jump! Sarah fumed to herself. *Just jump already! Jump and be done with it!* She could feel the eyes of the other parents on her little girl, eyes filled with pity, exasperation, smirking condescension. Sarah imagined those eyes turning on her, glaring into her shoulder blades. *Is that your daughter?* they'd ask, judging her.

Sarah debated whether she should go out there and *make* her jump. Maybe she'd up the bribe ante. Maybe she'd threaten to take away time with friends if she didn't. She'd scold her, *shame* her, into jumping. She began plotting the lecture she'd unleash afterward.

Then she saw Eric stand up and walk over to Heather. He leaned over and whispered in his daughter's ear, muffled by the hum of the swimmers and the lapping of the water. No one could hear a sound from him. He might've just been mutely mouthing the words.

When Eric was done, Heather nodded her head curtly, rapidly. Her father didn't walk back, but stood by the pool, turning his head to Sarah and giving her a quick wink. Heather unfolded her arms, bent her legs, and jumped.

When her head popped up above the water, she craned her neck upward to look at her dad, water streaming down her face and past her joyful, open grin. He smiled back and didn't say a word.

Afterward, when Heather and the other kids had gone to bed, Sarah asked Eric what he said.

Eric smiled. "I told her I'd be right there beside her. I wasn't going anywhere. And that if it looked like she was in any trouble at all, I'd go in after her."

Right there.

"I am with you and will watch over you wherever you go," God tells Jacob in Genesis, the very first book of the Bible (Genesis 28:15). It's a promise He makes again and again to His people. "I am with you," He tells us. "I'm right there."

He promised us His presence. He doesn't guarantee that He'll always be pleased with us. He doesn't promise a life of ease or comfort. But He doesn't insist that we earn His presence either. Jacob certainly wasn't perfect, and God knows we're not either. He understands our sins and weaknesses better than we do, and He knows we'll make mistakes. But when we agree to be part of His family, God promises that He'll be with us, standing, watching, smiling.

Right there. Maybe that's what parenting is all about in the end. Maybe the billions of words written on the subject, including the nearly sixty-five thousand or so I've added, could be distilled down to just two. *Right there.* We'll be there in the mess. We'll be there in the muck. We may not always say the exact right words or have the right plan of action or even do the right thing, because we're part of the mess too. But we can promise to be right there, not just to take up space in their lives, but as an advocate. A protector. A guide. A *savior.* Someone who will not just say, "I love you," but "I love you when no one else seems to, when you're at your most unlovable. I'll love you when you get an F in algebra and when you break curfew. I'll love you when I ground you, when I take away your phone, when we're screaming at each other in the car. I'll love you when you hate me, when you dump all my hopes and dreams for you in the toilet and pull the handle. I'll love you even when I don't want to. I'll love you in the midst of your own imperfections, and I'll love you in spite of mine. *I'll be right there.*"

It's terrifying to love someone. We lose sight of that in our poems and platitudes. At least, when we marry someone, we have a sense of what we're getting into. Before we say "I do," we have the option to say, "I don't want to." Not so with parents and children. We bring our babies home as strangers, and we hand them our hearts. We never get them back. Not really. They are ours, and we are theirs—no asterisks, no loopholes. How messy these relationships are. How painful they can be.

How beautiful.

God does His best work in the mess. His oceans roar with power, waves curling in on themselves in hues of blue and green. The stormy skies crackle and flash, deep rumbles rolling for miles. His creation isn't safe or clean; it is, however, glorious. It's in the heart of His creation that sometimes we see the Creator best. "I'm right there," He says in the swirling waves. *Right there* in the tempest. *Right there* even in the dirt and dust of a Zambian church camp, the sky filled with the voices of hurting, happy children.

God does His best work in *our* messes too. And families have the blessing of mess. It's thrilling and frustrating and frightening because it's real, perhaps the most real and most powerful thing we'll experience in our mortal lives. It's not perfect. *We're* not perfect. But maybe, even in the midst of its imperfection, family reflects something better. We see the heart of God in it. And through it, we're able to be part of God's story in a way that makes us laugh and cry and sing and sit, listening to the breath of the Almighty.

"I'm right there," God says in the family. It's an honor, a gift, to be right there too.

ACKNOWLEDGMENTS

Books, like families, aren't the products of just one person, and many helped with this one.

Thanks to Jean, Trent, and Troy for everything they are and for all they've done to make this book possible, from the stories we shared here to the support and grace they showed in letting me talk about them. I unpacked some raw, difficult times here, and it's not easy to expose these uncomfortable moments for the world to see and read about—especially when you're a teenager. Thanks, boys. Jean especially walked through this process with me story by story with patience and grace, sometimes helping me remember important details that I might've forgotten.

I'd also like to thank my writing collaborator, Paul Asay, for his talent and time in helping shepherd this book through this sometimes herky-jerky process. Focus on the Family's Jeanie Young and Don Morgan did a great job in finding and supplying some of the letters you read here, and the Focus on the Family Daily Broadcast team combed through hundreds of broadcast transcripts to help find the ones we used. And I owe a special word of thanks to those people whose own raw, beautiful stories helped flesh out the soul of this book.

Every author needs an editor, and I'm fortunate to have one of the best. Zondervan's John Sloan was instrumental in helping shape this project well before the first word hit the page. And once I had 65,000 of those words, John picked up his editorial scalpel and, through judicious cuts, tweaks, and suggestions, made them all better. Thanks to him, fellow editor Dirk Buursma, and all the folks at Zondervan for having faith in this book and seeing this project through. And finally, I'd like to give a special thanks to my agent, Wes Yoder—the wise, gentle force who helped give the book its graceful, godly DNA. This wouldn't have been possible without you, my friend.

NOTES

Chapter 1: Not Good Enough

1. See David Brooks, *The Road to Character* (New York: Random House, 2015), xi.
2. Cited in Nick Bilton, "Parenting in the Age of Online Pornography," January 7, 2015, www.nytimes.com/2015/01/08/style/parenting-in-the-age-of-online-porn.html?_r=0 (accessed January 4, 2017).
3. Cited in Michael Lipka, "Millennials Increasingly Are Driving Growth of 'Nones,'" May 12, 2015, www.pewresearch.org/fact-tank/2015/05/12/millennials-increasingly-are-driving-growth-of-nones (accessed January 4, 2017).

Chapter 2: What a Family Is

1. Rabbi Shmuel Goldin, "What God Has Joined Together," DVD session 6 of The Family Project.
2. Cited in Okmulgee News Network, "60 Percent of Women See Motherhood as Most Important Role," May 6, 2016, www.okmulgeenews.net/local-news/item/4267–60-of-women-see-motherhood-as-most-important-role (accessed January 4, 2017).
3. Eric Metaxas and John Townsend, "Mothers as Image-Bearers," DVD session 7 of The Family Project.
4. Ibid.

5. Cited in Ryan Sanders, "Kids Need Their Fathers: For Health, for Growth, for Life," July 5, 2012, www.fatherhood.org/bid/147397/Kids-Need-Their-Fathers-For-Health-For-Growth-For-Life (accessed January 4, 2017).

6. Carey Casey, "First Hero, First Love: A Dad's Role for Sons and Daughters," National Center for Fathering, www.fathers.com/s7-hot-topics/sons/first-hero-first-love-a-dads-role-for-sons-and-daughters (accessed February 1, 2017).

7. Tony Evans, "Fathers as Image-Bearers," DVD session 8 of The Family Project.

8. Cited in Institute for Social Research, University of Michigan, "Facebook Use Predicts Declines in Happiness, New Study Finds," August 14, 2013, http://home.isr.umich.edu/releases/facebook-use-predicts-declines-in-happiness-new-study-finds (accessed January 4, 2017).

Chapter 3: Broken or Real?

1. Leo Tolstoy, *Anna Karenina* (Cleveland: World, 1946), 15.

2. Alex Morris, "The Forsaken: A Rising Number of Homeless Gay Teens Are Being Cast Out by Religious Families," September 3, 2014, www.rollingstone.com/culture/features/the-forsaken-a-rising-number-of-homeless-gay-teens-are-being-cast-out-by-religious-families-20140903 (accessed January 4, 2017).

Chapter 4: The Fundamentals

1. See, for example, A. N. Meltzoff and M. K. Moore, "Imitation of Facial and Manual Gestures by Human Neonates," *Science* 198 (1977): 75–78.

Chapter 5: Opposites Attract

1. Linda Waite et al., *Does Divorce Make People Happy? Findings from a Study of Unhappy Marriages* (New York: Institute for American Values, 2002), http://americanvalues.org/catalog/pdfs/does_divorce_make_people_happy.pdf (accessed January 4, 2017).

2. See Erma Bombeck, *The Grass Is Always Greener over the Septic Tank* (New York: McGraw-Hill, 1976).

3. Jim Daly, *Marriage Done Right: One Man, One Woman* (Washington, D.C.: Regnery, 2016).

Chapter 6: Messy Lessons

1. Polly Klaas Foundation, "The Truth About Runaway Teens," www .pollyklaas.org/enews-archive/2013-enews/article-web-pages/the -truth-about-runaways.html?referrer=https://www.google.com/# .V3Ad35MrLSw (accessed January 4, 2017).

2. Cited in Alex Daniels, "Religious Americans Give More, New Study Finds," November 25, 2013, https://philanthropy.com/article/ Religious-Americans-Give-More/153973 (accessed January 4, 2017).

3. Cited in Giving USA, "2015 Was America's Most-Generous Year Ever," June 13, 2016, https://givingusa.org/giving-usa-2016 (accessed January 4, 2017).

4. Gallup editors, "Most Americans Practice Charitable Giving, Volunteerism," December 13, 2013, www.gallup.com/poll/166250/ americans-practice-charitable-giving-volunteerism.aspx (accessed January 4, 2017).

5. Minnesota Atheists, "Ten Things Christians Do Better Than Atheists—#1 Charity Work," http://mnatheists.org/news-and-media/ letters-and-essays/178–10-things-christians-do-better-than-atheists-1 -charity-work (accessed January 4, 2017).

6. Quoted in J. Patrick Lewis, *Michelangelo's World* (Mankato, MN: Creative Editions, 2007), 7.

7. Quoted in Pray Now Group, *Living Stones: Pray Now Weekly Devotions & Monthly Prayer Activities* (Edinburgh: Saint Andrew Press, 2015), 165.

Chapter 7: The Blame Game

1. Drs. Beverly and Tom Rodgers, *Becoming a Family That Heals: How to Resolve Past Issues and Free Your Future* (Colorado Springs: Focus on the Family, 2009).

Chapter 8: A Safe Place

1. See IndexMundi, "United States Age Structure," October 8, 2016, www.indexmundi.com/united_states/age_structure.html (accessed January 4, 2017).
2. See IndexMundi, "Zambia Age Structure," October 8, 2016, www .indexmundi.com/zambia/age_structure.html (accessed January 4, 2017).

Chapter 9: Accepting Free Will

1. C. S. Lewis, *The Great Divorce* (1946; repr., San Francisco: Harper SanFrancisco, 2001), 75.
2. Cited in Ed Stetzer, "Dropouts and Disciples: How Many Students Are Really Leaving the Church?" May 14, 2014, www.christianity today.com/edstetzer/2014/may/dropouts-and-disciples-how-many -students-are-really-leaving.html (accessed January 4, 2017).

Chapter 11: Transitions

1. Casey Baseel, "Japanese Man's Parents Present Notice of Expiration of Child-Rearing Services on 20th Birthday," October 8, 2015, http:// en.rocketnews24.com/2015/10/08/japanese-mans-parents-present -notice-of-expiration-of-child-rearing-services-on-20th-birthday (accessed January 4, 2017).
2. Cited in Randye Hoder, "Studies Find Most Teens Sext before They're 18," *Time* magazine, July 3, 2014, http://time.com/2948467/ chances-are-your-teen-is-sexting (accessed January 4, 2017).

ABOUT JIM DALY

Jim Daly is president and CEO of Focus on the Family and host of its National Radio Hall of Fame–honored daily broadcast, heard by more than 6.3 million listeners a week on more than 1,200 radio stations across the United States and by 85 million listeners worldwide.

Daly's personal journey from orphan to head of an international Christian organization dedicated to helping families thrive is a powerful story. Abandoned by his alcoholic father at age five, Daly lost his mother to cancer four years later—a wound deepened when his grieving stepfather emptied the family home and took off with almost everything while Daly, the youngest of five children, and his siblings were at their mother's funeral.

After being in foster care, Daly became a Christian in high school and found meaning, purpose, and a sense of belonging.

Daly assumed the presidency of Focus on the Family in 2005. He began his career at Focus in 1989 as an assistant to the president. In 2004, he was appointed chief operating officer, a role he held until he was handpicked by founder Dr. James Dobson to be the ministry's president.

Daly earned a BS in Business Administration in 1984 from California State University. After graduating, he worked in the private sector for a FORTUNE 500 company. In 1997, he completed his MBA in International Business at Regis University, and in 2009, he received an honorary Doctor of Letters degree from Colorado Christian University.

Daly has received the 2008 World Children's Center Humanitarian Award, the 2009 Children's Hunger Fund Children's Champion Award, and the 2010 HomeWord Family Ministry Award. His blog, "Daly Focus," appears online at jimdaly.focusonthefamily.com.

Daly is the author of six books: *Marriage Done Right*, *The Good Dad*, *ReFocus*, *Stronger*, *Finding Home*, and *When Parenting Isn't Perfect*. He and his wife, Jean, have two children and live in Colorado Springs.

ABOUT PAUL ASAY

Paul Asay is an award-winning journalist who wrote about religion for *The Gazette* in Colorado Springs. He has been published by such outlets as *The Washington Post, Christianity Today, Time,* and *Beliefnet .com.* The author of *God on the Streets of Gotham,* Asay is a senior associate editor at *Plugged In,* a ministry that reaches more than six million people with movie reviews that help people understand popular cultural trends and how they intersect with spiritual issues. His particular interest is the unexpected ways faith and media intersect. He lives in Colorado Springs with his wife, Wendy, and their two children.

ReFocus

Living a Life That Reflects God's Heart

Jim Daly, President of Focus on the Family, with Paul Batura

Written by the compassionate leader of Focus on the Family, *ReFocus* inspires and motivates Christians to transcend political agendas and partisan battles and instead interact with others in a way that will consistently reveal the heart of God to a desperately hurting world.

Our culture has become painfully polarized, often hindering relationships with neighbors, colleagues, and the very people who need to discover the love of Jesus. Remembering that we are citizens of heaven who serve a loving Father, we who call ourselves followers of Christ can once again be known by our love.

But how? In what context and through what means? How can we tear down the walls that divide our culture, neighborhoods, workplaces, and families in this increasingly contentious world?

Drawing on a rich variety of true stories and sources both historical and contemporary, Jim Daly challenges us to reclaim our responsibility and our privilege as God's sons and daughters.

Available in stores and online

The Good Dad

Becoming the Father You Were Meant to Be

Jim Daly, President of Focus on the Family, with Paul Asay

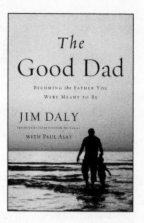

Jim Daly is an expert in fatherhood—in part because his own "fathers" failed him badly. His biological dad was an alcoholic. His stepfather deserted him. His foster father accused Jim of trying to kill him. All were out of Jim's life by the time he turned thirteen.

Isn't it odd—and reminiscent of the hand of God—that the director of the leading organization on family turned out to be a guy whose own background as a kid and son were pretty messed up? Or could it be that successful parenting is discovered not in the perfect, peaceful household but in the midst of battles and messy situations, where God must constantly be called to the scene?

Using his expertise, humor, and an inexhaustible wealth of stories, Jim will show you that God can make you a good dad in spite of your upbringing and in spite of the mistakes you've made. Maybe even because of them.

It's not about becoming a perfect father; it's about trying to become a better father, each and every day. It's about building relationships with your children through love, grace, patience, and fun—and helping them grow into the men and women they're meant to be.